The Declaration of Independence. *This is one of only t... copies of the Dunlap Broadside. It was discovered at a flea market in 1989. Two hundred broadsides were printed by John Dunlap in Philadelphia, Pennsylvania, on July 4, 1776. (Courtesy of Norman and Lyn Lear)*

DECI

SPEAK.
CONNECT.
ACT.
VOTE.

YOUR

MORE THAN 50 CELEBRATED
AMERICANS TELL YOU WHY

WITH AN INTRODUCTION BY
AMERICA FERRERA

GREENWILLOW BOOKS
An Imprint of HarperCollinsPublishers

Declare Yourself

Speak. Connect. Act. Vote. More Than 50 Celebrated Americans Tell You Why

Copyright © 2008 by HarperCollins Publishers.

Pages 324–325 constitute an extension of the copyright page.

All rights reserved. Printed in the United States of America. No part of this book may be used or reproduced in any manner whatsoever without written permission except in the case of brief quotations embodied in critical articles and reviews. For information address HarperCollins Children's Books, a division of HarperCollins Publishers, 1350 Avenue of the Americas, New York, NY 10019.

www.harperteen.com

The text of this book is set in 11-point Bell.

Book design by Paul Zakris

Library of Congress Cataloging-in-Publication Data

Declare yourself : speak, connect, act, vote : More than 50 celebrated Americans tell you why.

p. cm.

"Greenwillow Books."

ISBN 978-0-06-147332-6 (trade bdg.)

ISBN 978-0-06-147316-6 (pbk. bdg.)

1. Youth—United States—Political activity. 2. Political participation—United States. 3. Political culture—United States. 4. Popular culture—Political aspects—United States. 5. United States—Politics and government—2001–.

HQ799.2.P6D43 2008

323'.04208350973—dc22

2007049592

First Edition 10 9 8 7 6 5 4 3 2 1

 GREENWILLOW BOOKS

CONTENTS

CONTENTS

CONTENTS

CONTENTS

★ FOREWORD ★

One of the great pleasures of each generation is to
reimagine the world as a better place—and then to fight to
achieve it. I've often wondered how today's young people
will play out this hero's quest. An earlier generation of
Americans helped abolish slavery. Another won the vote
for women. Another helped usher in a new era of civil
rights and equal opportunity.

So what will young people make of their gifts from an
earlier era of Americans, these gifts known as the
Constitution and Bill of Rights? Will they be too plugged
in to iPods and video games to care, or will they outshine
earlier generations with bold new solutions to our many
national problems?

These thoughts frequently cross my mind because I am now, at age eighty-five, poised in the middle of five generations of family members whose lives will span more than two centuries of American life. My grandfather was born in 1868, and was a formative influence on my life in the 1930s—and now, I am sobered to think that my twenty-year-old son, two thirteen-year-old daughters, and four grandchildren, ages four to sixteen, will live to see the late twenty-first century, and *their children* will welcome in the twenty-second century! So how has, and will, each generation of the Lear family make its mark on its time?

My journey toward citizenship began when I was nine, when I was living with my grandfather in New Haven, Connecticut. We had lots of parades in those years—Veterans Day, Memorial Day, the Fourth of July, Presidents' Day—and I remember clutching his hand as we stood on street corners watching those parades as the color guard marched by and the martial music blared; inevitably a tear would start down his cheek and he squeezed my hand till it hurt.

I often stood at the kitchen table as he wrote the latest installment of a countless series of letters to the president of the United States. Each of them began, "My dearest darling Mr. President . . . " He praised the president for some decisions and chastised him for others—but in all cases, my grandfather let the president know that the presidential powers were being exercised in his name and the names of millions of fellow citizens. This is how I learned, as a nine-year-old boy, about the "consent of the governed" described in the Declaration of Independence.

From such experiences, I developed a visceral love of my country and a personal vigilance about the behavior of my elected officials. I proudly flew with the 15th Air Force over Germany in World War II, following which and ever since, I have participated in political campaigns and citizen protests. As a television writer and producer in the 1970s and beyond, I put together a company of like-minded writers, producers, and directors to stimulate debates about the great issues of our time as they played out around kitchen tables and living rooms in the TV shows we were presenting.

My life and career as a citizen took an unexpected turn in 2001 when my wife and I learned that one of the few surviving copies of the Declaration of Independence—the so-called Dunlop broadside—was up for sale. We jumped at the chance to acquire this rare document. From the start, we saw it as "The People's Document": in effect, our country's birth certificate. We didn't want to hang it on a wall somewhere. We wanted it to travel *everywhere* so that people could see it and reconnect to the core values and hopes that launched this country.

And so we created the Declaration of Independence

Road Trip, a traveling exhibit that toured schools and museums, businesses and town halls, the Olympics and NASCAR races, the Super Bowl and six presidential libraries. The Declaration eventually traveled to over fifty cities in thirty states. Young children gazed with awe at the document. I saw sailors on a battleship in New York Harbor get all choked up. Sometimes people waited two hours just to see it.

When the Road Trip concluded, we wondered what the Declaration of Independence might wish *us* to do to help advance its vision. The answer we intuited was: *celebrate the blessings of citizenship and voting*. At a time when voter participation was declining—only one-third of all young people voted in 2000, down from one-half of young people in 1972—we decided to promote voter registration. We established a new nonprofit, nonpartisan organization, Declare Yourself, and partnered with civic organizations, musicians, young actors, media companies, and many others to help us reach young people with a timely message: *Vote!*

A number of organizations, including Declare Yourself, were active throughout 2003 and 2004 in this mission. It was gratifying to see that the 2004 presidential election had the highest youth voter turnout ever, with more than twenty million young voters. Now we want to build on this momentum and reach out to even more young people to encourage them to vote in the 2008 elections and beyond and to discover the satisfaction of getting involved.

Voting is the gateway experience to a life of active citizenship. If you register to vote when you turn eighteen, you are far more likely to keep voting—and to take your responsibilities as an American citizen more seriously. And if you take yourself seriously as a citizen, you are more likely to help this nation fulfill the promise of the Declaration of Independence. You are more likely to participate in democratic debate, civic organizations, and electoral campaigns. You are more likely to pressure our elected leaders to serve us well.

If the United States of America is going to meet the challenges of the decades ahead, it will need all the citizen talent and energy that it can mobilize. The Declaration does not actualize itself. Our Constitution and Bill of Rights do not automatically generate freedom and responsible governance. Those outcomes require *us*, all of us.

What better way to explore these issues than to read the personal testimonials of prominent Americans from all walks of life? The pieces that you will read in this book— by Alice Walker, Adrian Grenier, Courtney E. Martin, Robert Ben Garant, and many others—explain in highly personal terms why voting matters. Contributors Holly Shulman, Megan McCafferty, and the rock band Maroon 5 describe how they have helped make our democracy work and how they envision democracy in the future.

This book should help you to see that we are all threads in a very large tapestry. One by one, we make our nation's history. Do you like freedom? Do you care about your family, your community, and the future? Then vote. Our nation depends on you. The great judge Learned Hand said it well: "Liberty lies in the hearts of men and women; when it dies there, no constitution, no law, no court can save it. . . . "

My generation has been called the "greatest generation" for its role in World War II. But I have every confidence that today's young people, as they grapple with the unprecedented challenges of their time, will seize that title for themselves. Which is exactly how it should be. My bet is that we have only begun to hear from the latest, greatest generation of young Americans. May this book help stimulate their vision and energy.

Now, read, express yourself with brutal candor, debate—and go vote.

NORMAN LEAR has enjoyed a long career in television and film, and as a political and social activist and philanthropist. A former television writer, he went on to produce many hit television shows and films, as well as found numerous nonprofit organizations, including People For the American Way, the Norman Lear Center at USC, and Declare Yourself. You can find out more at www.normanlear.com.

★ INTRODUCTION ★

This 2008 election belongs to our generation.
What happens this year determines our future. And
not in the cheesy, graduation-ceremony sense of
the word "future," but the literal, how our daily
lives will change kind of future.

It's easy to forget that a presidential election is in
fact not about the candidates, but about us. We are
voting for ourselves, and for one another. We are
choosing between bringing our friends and family
home, or keeping them at war for the next hundred

years. We are voting to give ourselves health care, or to accept the emergency room as the best we deserve. We are voting for a chance to afford college, for a chance at a decent job, for a chance to one day own a home. We're voting for the opportunity to save ourselves from an angry planet, to order sushi that's not contaminated with mercury, to drink water that won't make us sick, and to drive cars that won't keep us at war. This year when you go to the polls to cast your vote, you're not merely voting for politicians, you're voting for you.

Studies show that our generation cares intensely about positive change, and that we're willing to work for it. Already, as I write this in early 2008, the media is talking about the astonishing number of young people who have voted in the primaries, with many states recording numbers that doubled, tripled, or even quadrupled the 2000 and 2004 turnout.

Still, there's a fair amount of skepticism over whether we will maintain our enthusiasm and our engagement through November. Already, the media and the older demographics have started to question our commitment. I just finished reading an article online about how energized young voters are this year. But one reader responded to the article with this comment: "Every presidential election there's talk about the youth turning out in record numbers and changing things. Every presidential election they don't."

Okay, fair enough. For the past thirty-odd years, young voters have had a bad habit of getting all charged up, then not actually going to the polls.

It's also true that even when the youth vote spiked the way it did in 2004, the older generations beat us by a mile. Take a look: 47 percent of young people voted in the 2004 presidential election, but 73 percent of people in their 50s and 60s voted.

These numbers suggest that young people don't think about what's going on in their lives and around the world. I know this is simply not true.

I've traveled across the country during this campaign speaking to young people on college campuses, in vocational schools, in bars, and in coffee shops. What I discovered is that our generation cares intensely about the legacy it will leave behind. But what we must understand here and now is that if we want something to change, we must change something.

We have to turn apathy into action and see ourselves as a new generation. A different generation. After all, we're a wired generation. We've got YouTube and MySpace and Facebook, etc. We've got more ways of finding information and sharing information than ever before. Now we must use that information. We must be heard and be counted.

We must vote!

AMERICA FERRERA is a screen and stage actor best known as the star of TV's *Ugly Betty*, for which she has won an Emmy, Golden Globe, and Screen Actors Guild award. Her breakout role was in the independent film *Real Women Have Curves*, which lead to many more high-profile projects, including *The Sisterhood of the Traveling Pants* and its upcoming sequel scheduled to release in August 2008. Additional upcoming films scheduled for release in spring 2008 include *Under the Same Moon* and *Towards Darkness*, which she executive-produced through her production company, Take Fountain. The daughter of Honduran immigrants, America is also a student of international relations at the University of Southern California. She was named 2007's Hispanic Woman of the Year by *Hollywood Reporter* and *Billboard* magazine, and was also cited in *Time* magazine's "Time 100: The Most Influential People in the World." She is twenty-three years old. (Photo © MR Photo / Corbis Outline)

DECLARE YOURSELF

★ Maya Angelou ★

Why Voting Matters

One of the loneliest images I can bring to mind is that of a person without a country.

Americans at home and abroad are easily recognized because they walk, maybe even strut, with airs of confidence up and down the avenues of the world.

The attitude can be explained in the way Americans think.

"Yes, I can.

I am an American.

Yes, I can."

I believe that air comes from being able to vote. Each American feels that he or she has some authority over the laws and rules of our country.

We try to vote in the leadership we want, and to vote out those who displease us. Of course the majority will rule, which means there are winners and losers. Still, the voter who has not chosen the triumphant side knows that at least one vote has been cast for his or her choice.

The strength of the American would be drained from the proud shoulders, the lilt in the voices, and even the spring of the steps, without the right to vote.

The citizen who does not vote weakens herself and her country, slights her ability to be an American citizen and a citizen of the world. I am proud to try to vote in the leaders I like and try to vote out those who do not earn my approval.

Watch me as I walk up and down the streets of the world. Anyone who sees me must know that I am an American. I vote.

MAYA ANGELOU is a writer, professor, and actor, perhaps best known for her memoir *I Know Why the Caged Bird Sings*, as well as her poetry. Among her diverse accomplishments are her active role in the American civil rights movement, her writing and composing for television and film, and her reciting one of her poems at Bill Clinton's presidential inauguration.

★ TYRA BANKS ★

I remember the first time I voted like it was yesterday. I was eighteen years old. Fashion Week was in full swing in New York City, and I was literally running between the tents, through the chaotic world of models, makeup, and clothes. Supermodel Christy Turlington overheard me saying, "I need to go vote." I was not a supermodel at the time—I was working a lot and making a name for myself, but I didn't have supermodel status at the time like Christy. Christy grabbed me and said, "Tyra, let's go right now."

We didn't have much time before our next run-way walks. In fact, we were in full hair and makeup (and I mean crazy-outrageous–looking hair and makeup). I jumped into Christy's car (she had a limo waiting) and we made it to the polls. I remember walking into the voting booth, closing the curtain, and feeling an overwhelming sense of importance. I really felt like I mattered. I felt like I was partici-pating in my future and the future of our country.

I didn't walk into the voting booth blind. I had researched and read about the different candidates and the propositions that were in my little booklet. I wanted to make informed decisions. I made sure that, to the best of my ability, I had thought through every possible thing I had the opportunity to vote on. To me, voting is not just a privilege, it is a responsibility.

This upcoming election is so incredibly impor-tant. There are so many issues that need to be addressed—from the war, to the economy, to global warming, the list goes on and on. Now that I host a talk show that has millions of young people among its viewers, I've felt the responsibility to encourage my audience to vote, and to address issues that matter to them. When we first put the word out that we were interested in booking political candidates on the Tyra show, I wasn't sure if they would come. I'm not Diane Sawyer—and I've never claimed to be—but I do reach a specific audience of potential young voters who have the POWER to elect the candidate THEY want to be president.

I'm never really nervous before interviews. When big stars like Beyoncé have come on the show, I've gotten *excited*, but never that sweaty-shaky-hand-feel-it-in-my-stomach feeling that I got before interviewing Senator Barack Obama, who was the first candidate to come on my show. I think I was just anxious because I've never had such a historic political figure on the show before. I knew I had just one hour to get in all of the questions I had been thinking about (and to work in the questions my audience had e-mailed me), and I wanted to make a good impression, because this man could be our next president.

I was shaking when he first walked down my runway and sat across from me. I made him feel my shaky hand, and I think that actually calmed me down a bit. It's hard for me to believe that just a couple of years ago I was strutting down a runway. I can still hear some of the people who told me, "Tyra, you're just a model. No one will accept you as a talk-show host." I wanted to call up all those people and say, "You better watch Monday, because Senator Barack Obama is on the Tyra show!" He was amazing, personable, charismatic, and everything I had hoped he would be.

Senator Hillary Clinton came on the show soon after. And again, I was really nervous. She put me at ease because she was so real and vulnerable. I felt like I was chatting it up with an old friend. I asked her about how she had gotten through the toughest time in her life—how she had handled her husband's infidelity—and she answered me in such a real way, talking about how women come up to her and ask her for advice. Clips of that interview ran on *Good Morning America, Today, Entertainment Tonight,* and every cable news channel. I couldn't help but feel really proud. In a short amount of time I had come from wearing my drawers and Angels' wings on the runway to being taken seriously as a journalist.

Governor Mike Huckabee stopped by right after Hillary. He was charming and very likeable. I challenged him on a couple of issues (like gay rights) and he was fine going head-to-head with me. He even taught me to play electric guitar! I love it when candidates allow themselves to be seen as regular people. As I'm writing this now, John McCain looks like he'll be doing the Tyra show soon, too. I think it's important to hear what all of the candidates have to say, and learn a bit about who they are as real people, in order to make your best decision on election day.

I can't say it often enough: VOTE! It is a right that we cannot take lightly. It is a responsbility we must take seriously. This isn't about selecting your favorite Top Model. It's about your future. Whatever it is that you dream of pursuing in life can be affected by who takes the office of president. So make sure you do your research, and you get your butt into that voting booth! Do it!!!

TYRA BANKS is a former supermodel who hosts the reality show *America's Next Top Model* as well as her own Emmy-nominated *The Tyra Banks Show*. She has appeared in television shows and feature films such as *Felicity, The Fresh Prince of Bel-Air,* and *Coyote Ugly*. She has been repeatedly ranked among the world's most influential people by *Time* magazine. You can learn more at www.tyrabanks.com. (Photo courtesy of Warner Brothers)

★ BONNIE BERNSTEIN ★

Yep. I was just like you. "Why do I need to vote?" I'd ask myself on Election Day. Did I really feel like taking time out of my busy Tuesday to wait in line for who-knows-how-long, just to walk into a metal booth with a curtain and flip a bunch of levers to "let my voice be heard"?

"Nah," I'd always conclude. "Plenty of people will vote. No one will lose out if I don't."

And I'd bag it—every time.

Now don't get me wrong. I'm very interested in

politics. I started paying close attention in my senior year at the University of Maryland during the run-up to the 1992 elections, and also covered Bill Clinton's inauguration for my first job. I remember being so excited driving down to our nation's capital in my clunky white KIX-106 van with the big ol' cowboy boot painted on the side. I was twenty-two years old, working as the news and sports director at a tiny country radio station in Lewes, Delaware, and *I* was actually issued a credential for the presidential inauguration. What a great country!

I felt so patriotic that day standing on the National Mall, watching the forty-second president take the oath of office. I got chills listening to renowned poet Maya Angelou recite "On the Pulse of Morning," an original piece she wrote to commemorate the day.

Still, I failed to go to the polls in 1996 and 2000. And it wasn't until November 7, 2000, that I realized how monumental a mistake that was.

Early that election night, it appeared the race between Vice President Al Gore, the Democratic candidate, and George W. Bush, the Republican governor of Texas, had all but been decided. The exit polls were indicating—and the networks were announcing—that Gore had clinched Florida's twenty-five electoral votes, giving him the presidency. But right before I went to bed, I flipped on the TV again, only to see the networks waffling. Bush was now passing Gore in the polls. Did the networks prematurely award Gore the victory? There were still many ballots to be counted.

The next morning, the media was in a total frenzy. Bush's margin over Gore was less than a thousand votes! Over the next month, recounts, uncertainty, and legal battles would dominate Florida's political landscape. The term "hanging chad" became a fixture in pop culture, thanks to the flimsy punch-card ballots used by many counties in the Sunshine State. If voters didn't completely punch the rectangular chad next to their candidate of choice, the card reader didn't always count the vote. What a mess.

At the end of the day, it seemed that even though Gore won the national popular vote, Bush earned more electoral votes, and ultimately, the presidency. It was the first time since the late 1800s, and just the third time in American history, a candidate had won the Electoral College without seizing the vote of the majority. That's what made me realize EVERY VOTE REALLY DOES COUNT.

While technically, voting is a right afforded to every American citizen, I consider it more of a privilege—especially when you consider it took more than forty years for Congress in 1920 to ratify the Nineteenth Amendment that gave women the right to vote. You may not think your one vote makes a difference, but if you calculate how many people think *precisely* the way you do, you realize the numbers add up.

There's a part of me that regrets not casting my first presidential ballot until 2004. I guess it's because as an "educated consumer," I read about the issues, I watch the debates, and I have strong opinions about the candidates. I even know for whom I would have voted . . . had I just gone to the polls.

When I finally did vote that crisp November day in 2004, I vividly recall standing in the metal booth with the curtain closed behind me. As I pulled down the lever next to my candidate, I felt empowered. It was so amazing to exercise my right, in a nation of 300 million people, to help choose the next leader of the United States.

Oh, and in hindsight, I'm glad I saved my credential from the '93 inauguration. It means a whole lot more to me now!

BONNIE BERNSTEIN is a reporter and host for ABC Sports and ESPN with more than fifteen years' experience in both television and radio broadcasting. She began her career as the news/sports director for a radio station in Delaware and later made local television history at the NBC affiliate in Reno, Nevada, becoming the "Biggest Little City's" first-ever female weekday sports anchor. You can find out more about her at www.bonniebernstein.com. (Photo credit: G. Newman Lowrence)

★ Ryan J. Bingham ★

A Conversation with a Young Mayor

What made you realize the importance of voting?

I grew up in a very political family. My grandfather was a state legislator for twelve years, from 1980–1992. Those were the years that I was a child. At that time my mother was on the city council of my hometown, Torrington, Connecticut, and my aunt was a probate judge in a neighboring town. So during my early childhood and beyond I was exposed to politics and public service. My family always told me that it was important to vote because that was how I could ensure that my government would run the way I felt that it should. So, I would say I am lucky enough to have always known the importance of voting because I grew up surrounded by many politically active people.

What made you decide to become politically active?

Growing up in a political family I was always involved in politics, from knocking on doors for my mother's campaign to volunteering at a campaign headquarters. These experiences are what led me to major in government in college. However, what really got me to become very active was when I returned home from college and saw that my hometown had taken a turn for the worse. Crime was on the rise, our downtown was turning into a ghost town, and the mayor at the time was not communicating to the public.

So I began to ask questions about why crime was up and what was happening with our downtown area. The more I asked the more I realized that nothing was being done. Finally, I thought that the only way to make a positive change was to run for mayor myself and reverse the trend. I spoke with my family and some close friends, who all encouraged me, and in July of 2005 I started my candidacy. I took office in December of 2005, and was reelected in November of 2007 for a second term. The long and short of it is: when you decide to make yourself aware of what's happening in your community, state, or country, that's when you decide to become politically involved.

What one issue is so important to you that you can't help but get involved with it and speak out about it through your vote?

One issue that gets me stirred up is when government enacts laws that can potentially harm one's personal freedom. Personally I believe that it is the right of all Americans to act as they wish, so long as it does not harm another person. Oftentimes government can punish people for acting in a certain manner—for example, why should we be taxed on gasoline because we need to drive to work? That's why when I vote I make sure the people I support feel the same way as I do. It's critically important to me to understand what decisions my leaders are making on all levels so that I have an idea how they will represent me if they win.

Is voting a right or a privilege? Is it an obligation or a choice? Why?

I think that voting is all those things. It is a right that is due to all citizens over eighteen. It is a privilege that our forefathers fought and died for at the very beginning of our country. Because of the debt we owe to those who sacrificed so that we may exercise our right to choose our government, it is an obligation. Most of all it is a choice; we must choose to vote because that is our democratic system of government. As citizens we can be as active or inactive as we wish. Personally, I choose to be an active participant because government affects basically all facets of life in this country.

What rights of being an American citizen do you hold especially dear? Why?

The first ten amendments of the United States Constitution are all very important and dear to me because they are the original rights that our founding fathers intended Americans to have. They are extensive and greatly encompassing. Two of the biggest rights for me as a citizen are the freedom of speech and the right to privacy. I feel these rights are so important because they allow us all as Americans to be individualistic. Other countries encourage extremes of conformity; however, our government says the opposite: that we are all different and should learn to coexist and accept those differences.

Do you have a great story of a friend or family member who got to vote for the first time?

The first time that my mother, Anne Ruwet, ran for state representative for the 65th district seat in Connecticut, she won by *one vote*. That one vote really could have been anyone, but one person sticks out in my mind. Our very good friend, who was around fifty years old, decided for the first time in his life to register to vote. For so long he had sat dormant and didn't care too much for politics and voting, but the first time he voted, he realized the power of his vote. Every vote matters. You wouldn't think that out of thousands of people who vote during elections that your vote matters. Look at my mother's story and the many other very close elections on all levels that are affected by just a few votes. It's an incredible opportunity to effect change or continue on a desired path!

Do you have any family history that makes you realize how important it is to not take your vote for granted now because of the struggles they went through for you?

One story comes to mind. As I stated earlier, my mother has been involved in politics her whole life, and in 2002 she decided to run for the state legislature. The incumbent had decided to retire and the seat was open. My mother and her challenger faced off in a heated election. In the end, my mom won the election by a single vote. Had two people decided to stay home she would have lost. It was strange when the final numbers came in that night because I remember thinking: if we had made one less phone call, missed one door, had one less sign out there, the outcome would have been completely different.

That story always reminds me about why voting is so important. The best thing about voting is that it opens the door to government. Once you do that, there is an entire world to discover where the work you do affects people's lives and if you do the right thing you can actually make positive change and help so many. Voting allows you to express your thoughts on government. I am thankful we worked so hard in 2002. If we hadn't, I might not have decided to run for mayor and I would not have accomplished so many positive things for my hometown.

How do you define patriotism?

George William Curtis once wrote, "A man's country is not a certain area of land, of mountains,

rivers, and woods, but it is a principle; and patriotism is loyalty to that principle." I believe that this sentence embodies my feelings on patriotism.

RYAN JOSEPH BINGHAM was elected mayor of Torrington, Connecticut, in November 2005. Voted in at twenty-two years old, he is the youngest mayor in the history of Connecticut. He grew up in Torrington and attended local schools. Mayor Bingham attended Marist College, where he received a BA in Political Science. He is currently serving his second term as mayor. (Photo credit: Sonja Zinke)

★ MEG CABOT ★

GIRLS RULE

GIRLS RULE.

At least that's what the T-shirts say.

But girls don't. Rule, I mean.

Personally, I don't care what sex the person is. . . . I just want whoever is in charge to be qualified for the job.

But I worry a little about those T-shirts. I worry because . . . well, you can't just put words on a T-shirt and assume what they say is true. Especially in light of the fact that they're not. Three-quarters of the women in the world are illiterate and are dependent on men for their livelihood. Girls definitely do not rule.

Even in our own country, women earn only sixty-nine cents for every dollar a man earns. Sixty-nine cents! Girls definitely do not rule here, either.

And yet, the T-shirts.

What gives, girls? A lot of us are wearing the shirts (I admit it. . . . I have one. They're cute!), but meanwhile, a recent poll found that only twenty-nine out of one hundred women in America consider themselves feminists.

I guess I could understand that if the definition of feminist was what I think a lot of the women who took that poll believed it to be . . . a hairy-legged, bra-burning, makeup-eschewing, man-hating woman who despises children and lives in a commune in the woods.

But that isn't what a feminist is. A feminist is a

person who favors political, social, and economic equality with men.

What's so wrong with that? That's not about girls ruling. That's about girls being on equal footing with the guys. Sounds good to me.

To me, a feminist is a person who, like me, shaves her legs, has lots of pretty Agent Provocateur bras, frequently visits the Clinique counter, loves men (well, most of them), loves other people's kids (when they aren't misbehaving in restaurants), thinks communes are very nice (for other people to live on), and hates the woods (except to look at from a distance).

In other words, a woman who just wants the same educational, social, and economic opportunities for women as for men.

I have heard some people say that they are not feminists because they don't believe it's necessary, due to the fact that men and women are treated equally in our country. Maybe they think the sixty-nine-cents-for-every-dollar thing could never happen to them.

Well, at the rate this country is going, it not only could, it probably *will* happen to them . . . and I'm scared for them! Unless we do something now to make a change, what happened to me one summer twenty years ago, way before I was a best-selling novelist, when I worked for Sears as a temp (through Manpower—get it? MANpower?), will happen to you—and I don't want it to!

My job was to move wet/dry vacs from one end of the store to the other, put up shelves to display them on, and paint the shelves. I was paid minimum wage, and felt lucky to be getting it, as jobs at the time were scarce in my town.

There were about ten women in my group, all doing the same job. And there was also a big group of men doing the EXACT SAME JOB.

I probably don't have to mention the fact that we ladies did the job better, faster, and more efficiently than the men. We got more wet/dry vacs moved, and more shelves built and painted, every day than the men did. Period.

Then came payday. And one of the women got a look at one of the men's paychecks and saw that he was getting two dollars more per hour than we were. Two dollars more an hour, for doing the EXACT SAME JOB that we ladies were doing (better than the men were).

We women were, understandably, furious. For one thing, a lot of the ladies in my group were single moms who had kids to feed and rent to pay. The only man in their life that they felt they could depend on was our boss—MANpower.

Whom we'd just learned was screwing us.

So we called Manpower on the spot and demanded they come over and take action IMMEDIATELY.

Which they did (come over, anyway). When we told them we were doing the EXACT SAME JOB as the men, only getting paid two dollars an hour less for it, they said to us, and I quote: "Well, yeah, but they're guys. We can't get guys to work for minimum wage, like we can you ladies."

We filed a complaint and eventually got MAN-power to retro-pay us one dollar more per hour for the work we'd done. ONE DOLLAR MORE. But it was a huge pain, and afterward, the Sears people didn't treat us very well, because they were so mad at us for complaining. Which is when I quit, because, um, excuse me, one dollar more per hour when the guys were still getting two?

Sadly, the ladies I worked with didn't have the luxury of being able to quit. They had bills to pay. I was just trying to finance a trip to Europe.

Still, you can see how my brush with sexism scarred me.

The thing that bothers me most about all this is that my mom and lots of women in her generation—not to mention those ladies back in the wet/dry-vac section at Sears—fought really hard so that women of my generation (and yours) could have the same jobs for the same pay as men.

And now those rights are slipping away from us, little by little, and the men (and one woman) of the Supreme Court are the ones who are allowing those rights that our mothers fought for to erode. We can't let that happen.

The thing is, if we choose to stay home and raise kids, like my mom did, that is totally our prerogative. But it's because of women like my mom and her friends that we HAVE that prerogative, and that we AREN'T one of the three-quarters of the women in the world who are illiterate: before, it was just a GIVEN that that was what we'd do—stay home and raise the kids. We can't let the leaders in Washington choose that kind of life for us.

Here's what it's NOT about: whether or not you wear a bra (or a GIRLS RULE T-shirt). If you don't want to wear a bra, you don't have to. But if you do want to—like a really cute pink polka-dotted one from Agent Provocateur—you totally can.

Here's what it IS about: being treated fairly. It's about making the same amount of money as men for the same work. It's about not letting men make our health decisions when they do not even own the equipment they're making those decisions about.

So, put your money where the words on your T-shirts are, girls (and any guys out there who are reading this who happen to like girls, and have the foresight to realize that what happens in the voting booth is going to affect what happens in your bedroom someday):

Get out there and vote.

And if you don't like anything I just said . . . hey, vote against me. That's your right, too. For now.

MEG CABOT is the author of nearly fifty books for both adults and teens, many of which have been best-sellers, most notably The Princess Diaries series, which has sold over five million copies worldwide. Meg, along with her cats and her husband, divides her time between Key West, Indiana, and New York City. Visit her online at www.megcabot.com. (Photo credit: Ali Smith)

★ NICK CANNON ★

YOUR VOTE COUNTS BECAUSE . . .

One of the main reasons I vote is because of what it represents. Voting is vital because it represents choices. Much of our lives is spent making choices, some insignificant, some of major importance. We choose what issues are important to us and vote on them in the hopes voting will make a difference in our lives and set standards for the future. At a certain point it is no longer acceptable just to sit around and complain about what is wrong with our neighborhoods, our cities, or our country if we run from the polls, "forget to vote," or pretend voting has nothing to do with us. Voting is not a burden or a job, it is a privilege. Every vote is important, every vote matters, and every vote counts.

I can remember being younger and a bunch of my friends talking about voting. I felt a little out of place because *everyone* was planning on voting (and I mean everyone), and they were all old enough to vote, except for me (let me reiterate, *everyone*). I knew at that moment that as soon as I turned eighteen and could vote, I was making it happen. I was going to vote for whatever there was to vote on: president, senator, governor, councilperson, proposition. . . . It didn't matter what it was, I was voting. It would be the first time, but not the last.

I wanted to vote, and I figured out a way to make voting fun. Aside from it being my right and my duty, it was another step in this big game of LIFE. Ironically enough, voting becomes even more significant when what I vote for wins. It is a feeling of accomplishment, as though I was the deciding factor in making something big happen. I helped make the decision, and at the end of the day, I am the winner. Voting is a step in the right direction. It is one of the easiest ways to make a societal impact, and better than most, because you don't have to do it alone.

My vote counts because *I* count. Your vote counts because YOU count. Together, WE count.

Make sure your vote gets counted!

NICK CANNON is a comedian, actor, and producer. He is the creator and executive producer of MTV's *Wild N' Out* and *Short Circuitz*, as well as the owner and creative director of the urban luxury line PNB Nation. The Cannes Film Festival named him "Breakthrough Actor of the Year" for his role in the film *Bobby*, the first time an African American has ever received this honor. Visit him online at www.nickcannon.com.

★ SASHA COHEN ★

I've represented the United States many times in international figure skating competitions, including the World Championships and the Olympics. When I saw the American flag hanging from the arena rafters or heard "The Star-Spangled Banner" being played, I would get a chill down my spine. I would think of the Statue of Liberty, which has given hope to so many. And I would be grateful for the opportunities I was given as an American, which inspired me to go after my dreams and to persevere against many odds.

But as I met people from other countries at those international competitions, I realized that, in America, we sometimes take our most basic rights for granted. I discovered that, in some countries, people aren't allowed to vote or their votes didn't count. For them, voting is simply a dream, while to you and me, it's reality. And for other people, who only recently got the right to vote, the idea of casting a ballot was absolutely thrilling.

In the United States, voting seems so ordinary. It's easy to think of it as just another chore, like changing the oil in your car. You know it's a good thing to do, but you find it kind of dull. And because voting is so matter of fact, it's also easy to think that it's not that important. In fact, you hear people say that all the time: "Oh, my vote won't count" or "One vote won't mean much when millions of people are voting." However, one vote *can* make a difference, especially in local elections for city council members and state representatives where not as many people vote. In those elections, people sometimes win literally by one vote. Even in presidential campaigns, if a candidate loses one county by a few hundred votes, he or she can lose the whole state, which may in turn mean losing the election.

I know that in the middle of a busy life filled with school, work, family, and friends, it's hard to find time to read about the issues, listen to the candidates, and get to the polls on Election Day. It's tempting to let other people take charge of everything—from choosing our president to raising taxes to build a new school. It's comforting to think that all these important questions will be sorted out without our input.

But think about it: every time you cast a vote, you're claiming your right to shape the world you live in. You're claiming your right to say how your tax dollars should be spent, how children and the elderly should be treated, how justice should be served, how we should protect the environment, and much more. You're claiming your right to make your vision of America—not somebody else's—into a reality.

Why would you hand over that right to other people? I truly believe that our generation will lead, create, and define the future. So let's all vote. Because every voice and every vote makes a difference.

SASHA COHEN is a professional figure skater who has won three World Championship medals—two silvers and one bronze—along with an Olympic silver medal, one U.S. title, and four U.S. silver medals. Outside of the rink, her activities include acting in television and film, charity work, and product endorsements. Find out more at www.sashacohen.com. (Photo © Lee Marshall Management)

★ LAUREN CONRAD ★

For me voting is much more than a choice. It's a right, and my responsibility. When I turned eighteen, it was the first time I felt like an adult. I felt like I had a say, and that my opinion was valued by others. It is easy to feel a little powerless growing up, with no way of doing anything that says to everyone, "Here's what I think." But as soon as you turn eighteen, you get the power to determine what happens in your world—your town, your state, your country. When I cast a vote, I am making a decision, the best one I can, about who I want to help lead our country. At eighteen, my vote counts as much as anyone else's. At eighteen, the choices I make are my own. When I registered to vote, I was given that power. And it is a lot of power.

I'm twenty-one and I've only been an adult for a few years now, but already I can see how important the choices I make are. I try to make sure I know as much as I can about any situation before I form an opinion.

When it is time to vote, I know that it is my responsibility to show up at the polls and make a decision. No one will be in charge of or be responsible for that decision but me. My friends can try to influence my choice of a candidate, but ultimately, the choice is mine and only mine.

To be part of this process, it's important to be informed and to know who stands for what. At the same time, it's really easy to get intimidated and confused by all there is to read in print, online, and in blogs; by all there is to see in debates, in videos, and at rallies. Even though it seems like a lot of work, even though it may be tempting to skip it, voting is a responsibility and a right and something we absolutely need to do. You can't tell yourself, "No one's going to notice just one vote; it doesn't matter if I don't show up." There's far too much at stake.

I take voting seriously because I understand that what we say matters…that the choices we make matter. A really important choice I made was to register and vote. I hope that you, your friends, and all young people make the same choice. Choose to register. Choose to study the issues. Choose a candidate who represents your point of view. If you don't have a point of view, get one. Take responsibility for yourself and for the future. Together we can choose to make our voices heard.

LAUREN CONRAD is the star of the MTV reality show *The Hills*. She has interned at *Teen Vogue,* and has her own fashion line, Lauren Conrad Collection. She received the Teen Choice Award for female reality TV star in 2006 and 2007. She is from Laguna Beach, California, and lives in Los Angeles.

★ CHRIS CRUTCHER ★

When I was in grade school my father offered me ten dollars if I could write to a million by ones. He wanted me to know what a big number that was. In those days you couldn't spend a million dollars in a lifetime. Mickey Mantle earned one-tenth of a million dollars per year playing baseball for the New York Yankees and he was the highest-paid player in the game. It was pretty much believed that the Mick couldn't spend all that money in a year if he treated his teammates to dinner at a different restaurant every night.

I sat down and started writing. By the time I got to a hundred, I figured my dad had blown ten big ones this time. At a thousand I was sure of it. By two thousand I began thinking it might take a few days, but ten bucks back then would buy a lot of Neccos. At ten thousand I realized that the number of digits I had to write for each number would continue to increase, that for the last nine hundred thousand numbers, I'd be writing six digits per. It seemed less and less like a good idea. Then it seemed like a bad idea. Then I quit. The exercise had its desired effect. I learned a million was a lot.

All of this backfired later in ways my dad might not have imagined, because another thing my father stressed throughout my youth was *responsibility*. To my father, a former World War II bomber pilot and a true patriot, one responsibility we all had after the age of twenty-one was to vote. He had fought and nearly died for his democracy and he wanted everyone, particularly his kids, to pay respect to that by participating in it. I did vote locally every year after I turned twenty-one because my mailing address was at my parents' and my father always ran for public office. He and I shared striking differences in perspective, but I voted for him because it gave him a job that would let him keep his house and car, and my mother in the style to which she had become accustomed. He could have been Stalin and he'd still have gotten at least one vote. Mine.

That was the last time I really thought my single vote counted. I moved to the San Francisco Bay Area, where suddenly no one was looking over my shoulder to make me responsible, and in that larger setting began to remember how many a million was. I was surrounded by many millions. In a national election there were hundreds of millions. I couldn't see that my one vote mattered. I had never witnessed an election where the difference between winning and losing was one vote.

Then one election afternoon in 1980 I was riding home from work, with the intention of stopping to vote, when the newscaster on my car radio told me my presidential candidate had already lost. Votes had been counted in the East and reported in the news. Not only did my one-in-a-million vote not mean much, it meant nothing.

I took my lament back to my father in Cascade, Idaho, during my next vacation and he gave me that same sad, how–did–you–get–switched–at–birth look I had seen nearly every day of my life growing up. "You think your responsibility begins and ends when you pull the curtain and put an x in a square? Vote that way and you're right. It doesn't mean a thing. You have to learn about the issues. You have to decide which ones matter to you and talk them up. You have to create a voting block, or join one. Voting doesn't just mean taking a half hour out of your day a couple of times a year."

I don't think my father and I voted the same on any single candidate from the time I reached voting age until the day he died, and you could probably count on one partially amputated hand the number of times we agreed on a political issue. But he was right. This country didn't get out of Vietnam because a few disgruntled voters went to the polls and voted. They got together and talked. They demonstrated. They created a huge block. It took time and lives were lost in that time, but the job got done. The Christian Coalition, with whom I almost never agree, is smart. They get their folks together and they create a hell of a block, pun intended, and the only way to fight them off is to create just as big a block on the other side.

Democracy isn't easy. It's cumbersome and the results can be disappointing. But the public discourse that comes from doing what we have to do to make our votes *count* makes us all smarter. I'm sixty-one years old as I write this. I have different issues than you may have just coming into adulthood. If the draft comes back, I'm way out of range. If we decide to do what I consider to be stupid things with Social Security, hey, I've got book royalties. Screw it up all you want to. If we vote to do little or nothing about global warming because it costs corporations too much, hey, like I said, I'm sixty-one. I'll be out of here before you're breathing through an oxygen mask. But none of that is true for you. I have more years to look back on than to look forward to, and I'd like to leave the country, and the planet, better than I found it. But I need to hear your voices so I can make good decisions on what that means. So get smart, loud, convincing. I'll join your voting block.

CHRIS CRUTCHER is the critically acclaimed author of eleven books, including *Staying Fat for Sarah Byrnes* and *Deadline*. He has won three lifetime achievement awards for his body of work. He has been a child and family therapist, and is currently chairperson for the Spokane Child Protection team. He lives in Spokane, Washington. Visit him online at www.chriscrutcher.com. (Photo credit: Kelly Halls)

★ ROSARIO DAWSON ★

Your voice is never too small, and you are never
too young to make a difference.

I know everyone says things like this, and that
they're hard to really believe. It's easy to be cynical,
especially when your life is not the cookie-cutter
American dream you see on TV or in the movies.
My life certainly wasn't. But then I saw the example my parents set for me and realized that my
power was real.

When I was young my parents chose to squat in

an abandoned building on the Lower East Side of Manhattan that had been neglected by the city for decades. My dad used his experience as a carpenter and my mom learned skills like plumbing and electrical to create a home. Their tenacity showed me how to use my own unique talents and self-respect to make things happen for myself *and* for other people. That's because our home did more than just shelter us: it was a haven for many of my friends and neighbors. Strangers came together from all over the world in my East Village New York, and with block parties, community gardens, and good old-fashioned daily outreach, the neighborhood thrived. I grew up watching people with less than average resources build a community.

That's how I know we all can make a difference.

And that's why I became a cofounder of Voto Latino. After learning that fifty thousand American Latinos turn eighteen each month, I thought, *These kids could be unstoppable.* My family, friends, and community inspired me to be proactive, and through them I know that voting can make the difference. But did the hundreds of thousands of young Americans coming of age in this country know that? Did they understand how much power they have?

The power to vote! It is Voto Latino's goal that they—YOU—do. You may not realize it, but you already vote every day . . . by not voting. When you don't vote, you let other people make choices and decisions for you; choices and decisions that directly affect your life. Voto Latino goes to where *you* are— on the Internet and on cell phones—and gives *you* the power to network online and register yourself and others. Utilizing these technologies gives you and your voice access and political power on your own time. (It also eliminates unnecessary paperwork—which helps keep the environment green!)

This isn't just a Latino issue; it's an American

issue. We all need one another to make a difference. AIDS, abuse, poverty, homelessness, health care, immigration, artists' rights, the environment, education: these are the issues that have made me mad or excited since I was a kid. They directly affect me and the people I care for, and they are prevalent in all our lives. I use my interests and personal experiences to give me a strong, knowledgeable voice— one that the politicians who work for *us* need to hear and be held accountable to. That's what your vote needs to be from you.

The face of America is changing, and our politics should reflect it. My heritage—Puerto Rican, Afro-Cuban, Native American, and Irish—is a mix of different histories and cultures coming together to be, in me, even stronger, just like our whole country. You too have a unique history, giving you an important voice that only you can share. And it needs to be heard.

What do you envision for yourself and your community, now and in the future? What kinds of things do you care about, and how does the government affect them? What issues are you passionate about? What are your dreams?

I dream of a day when everyone is enfranchised and true democracy is reached. But to get to that day, we all need to get out there—to vote, to participate in our communities and our government, and to make our voices heard. The best way to make a difference is by registering to vote, by learning who is running for office, both regionally and nationally, and by making sure that the candidate that you vote for is representing you.

This is *our* country. Represent!

ROSARIO DAWSON is an actor, producer, writer, and activist. She made her acting debut in *Kids*, and has since starred in films such as *Sin City*, *Rent*, and *Descent*, the last of which she produced with her production company, Trybe Films. She cowrites *The Occult Crimes Taskforce*, a comic book series, and is the cofounder of Voto Latino, a nonprofit organization that works to promote an enfranchised America by leveraging celebrity voices, the latest technology, and youth themselves to promote positive change. (Photo credit: Sheryl Nields)

★ CHRIS DEWOLFE ★
&
★ TOM ANDERSON ★

From the beginning, MySpace has always been primarily about individuality and self-expression. Each user has the opportunity to create a page that expresses who he or she is and what he or she believes in a very personal way. For the MySpace generation, voting has become an important continuation of their self-expression. This generation knows it has a voice, and it wants that voice to be heard.

As we watched MySpace grow, we noticed there

was a huge level of political interest, engagement, and activism among our members. As we generally let the MySpace community dictate the most relevant extensions and programs to offer, it seemed only natural to create some sort of official political/civic presence on the site. We wanted to create a political community where users could interact with politicians in a different format and on a different playing field than is normally available to younger or newer voters. The youth vote is always something that is talked about and never easily achieved; our goal was to bring both sides to the table in the hope that we could create a tipping point. Already this year young people have turned out and engaged in record numbers, and the power of social networking has helped the participation. Through MySpace Impact (impact.myspace.com), users are able to engage in political discussion; post blog entries, videos, and comments; and connect directly with the presidential campaigns. Conversely, every presidential candidate has the unique ability to connect with more than seventy million active members of the MySpace community. This is clearly not politics as usual.

The energy we have witnessed in this election season encouraged us to expand to an offline format. In 2007 MySpace Impact partnered with MTV to produce the "MySpace/MTV Presidential Dialogues." The forum provided an interactive and informative approach that put young people in charge of shaping the discussion. The questions were unfiltered and user-generated, and the candidates were candid and direct. The dialogues were successful because this generation is making a point to show up, be heard, and take control of its future in this country. Young people want to be an important part of this election, and we want to provide them the space to do so—we want to encourage and empower the youth of this country to vote. If all this excitement and energy translates to votes on Election Day, then we have done our job.

But, as usual, we think our users say it best:

★　★　★

My plea to you is this . . . just get out and vote. Do your research, make your voice heard. Vote for who YOU want and let your vote count. Don't rely on the opinion of others. It is your vote. —Mdufer, New Hampshire

★　★　★

Thank you . . . to the Best and most powerful page on MySpace! Everyone together . . . REGISTER AND VOTE . . . SPEAK OUT . . . It is our privilege, our right, it is what people have fought and died for in our past . . . Let us have that mean something. It's our responsibility . . . Bring our troops home . . . PEACE. —Seannie, Nevada

★ ★ ★

I always vote. I refuse to be one of those people who sit around complaining yet never do anything to make a difference. I really support what you are doing here. Wishing you the best and that everyone in our country of age would register and VOTE! Every vote is a vote for democracy . —"Wicked Wanda," Virginia

★ ★ ★

This is such a great site. I have been forwarding it to my friends who I know aren't registered to vote. Every vote counts! Everyone needs to vote! I don't care who you vote for because this is a democracy (even though it's obvious who I'd LIKE you to vote for). But, VOTE ANYHOW!!! —Lori, Indiana

CHRIS DeWOLFE and **TOM ANDERSON** are the founders of the social networking site and Internet phenomenon MySpace.com. Chris attended the University of Washington and the University of Southern California. Tom attended the University of California, Berkeley, and the University of California, Los Angeles. They created MySpace in 2003, and currently serve as its CEO and president, respectively.

★ KAT DELUNA ★

Like many people in this amazing country, I'm a child of immigrants. I was raised by a single mom from the Dominican Republic. She was always struggling to make ends meet for me and my sister, living in the Bronx and Newark for most of our lives.

I was lucky enough to be accepted to a performing arts high school where I was given opportunities most kids never get. I was exposed to all kinds of music and music history, and was lucky enough to study opera for years. Unfortunately, not all of my friends had the same arts education.

Part of the reason I am able to do what I love for a living is because of the opportunities I had growing up. Now I worry that one day we might live in a world where arts programs are seen as an "unnecessary expense."

Some may feel that in the grand scheme of things, with all of the war and conflict around us in the world, it may not seem important to make sure that kids have musical instruments, art supplies, great teachers, and dance classes—but it's important to *me*.

This is why voting can make such a difference. Voting allows for us to express our opinions on the things that matter most to us. The first time I voted I felt such a sense of empowerment and pride.

I know I'm only nineteen now, but I don't like to think of it that way. I'm nineteen! I have a lot of responsibility on my shoulders to make decisions that will affect my future and the future of the next generation. You can't just think of each election as something that will only affect the next four or eight years. It's more important and bigger than that, because whoever is running the country for that period of time is going to make decisions that will have very long-lasting results.

It's very easy to sit back and think that your vote doesn't count. It's easy to ignore the news, tune out all the politics, and simply sit on the sidelines with no opinion. I've always tried my best to resist saying "it doesn't matter what I think, I can't make a difference," because with everything going on today, and our country at war, that's just plain irresponsible.

I urge all young people to take advantage of our right to vote, to make your voice heard: it really makes a difference.

KAT DeLUNA is a rising star in the music world, with a sound that blends styles ranging from hip-hop to Latin jazz. She has performed on MTV's *TRL*, ABC's *Live with Regis and Kelly*, CBS's *The Late Late Show with Craig Ferguson*, and NBC's *Miss Teen USA*. Visit her online at www.katdeluna.com. (Photo credit: Michael Brandt)

★ ROBERT BEN GARANT ★

The first time I voted, I was nineteen, I had
just moved to New York City, the East Village, and
I had a green Mohawk. This is a true story, by the
way. I got in line to vote, at a school on Avenue B,
and accidentally stood next to a dude with a safety
pin through his nose, an anarchy T-shirt, and a *red*
Mohawk. He was pretty big. In New York, in the
eighties, there were all kindsa punk codes: red
braces (suspenders) meant one thing, yellow shoe-
laces meant something else, skins hated punks who

hated SHARPs. . . . It was very complicated, and I was fresh off the boat from Tennessee, so I wasn't sure—do red Mohawk guys get along with green Mohawk guys? Are they sworn enemies?

I don't know why, maybe I was all cocky 'cause I was voting or something, but I pointed out to him that if he was a true anarchist, he wouldn't be voting.

He pointed out to me that it was laundry day, he had only one clean T-shirt, and the message he sends with his T-shirt isn't as important as the message he sends by voting.

Looking back, I was lucky that day—twofold. 1: Those are kinda words to live by. And 2: He didn't break my nose. I sorta had it coming. And if I had gotten my nose broken the first time I went and voted . . . I don't know if I woulda voted again.

ROBERT BEN GARANT is an actor, comedian, writer, producer, and director. He is the cocreator, along with frequent collaborator Thomas Lennon, of the television show *Reno 911*, on which he plays the role of Deputy Travis Junior. The pair have cowritten screenplays for many hit films. Ben Garant got his start with The State, a comedy troupe that had its own show on MTV. (Photo credit: Daniel Longmire)

PEAK.CONNECT.ACT.VOTE

★ ANASTASIA GOODSTEIN ★

I spent the first two years of high school rebelling. I broke every rule I could at the girls' school my parents sent me to until the school finally asked me to leave. I dyed my hair blue-black, wore lots of vintage and big boots. I listened to fast, loud, angry hard-core punk music and fully embraced the mantra of sex, drugs, and rock and roll. Junior year, my parents sent me to high school number three, a private school with a reputation for being more liberal. It took. The approach of treating the high school students a lot like college students worked for me. When I was treated with respect and given trust, I lost my motivation to abuse it.

Around that time, I happened to pay attention to an episode of *20/20* my parents must have been watching. Hugh Downs was talking about how we were destroying the environment. I was riveted . . . moved . . . inspired to act. For the first time in my teenage life, I cared about something besides myself. Recycling was just beginning to catch on in Nashville, Tennessee, where I grew up in the eighties. I enlisted my BFF, Lizzie, as my lieutenant, and we decided to make recycling our cause, along with being vegetarians and not shaving our legs. We went through the steps of forming an official school environmentalist club and convinced our chemistry teacher to be our adviser. We enticed our peers to join with promises of hiking and rafting trips designed to connect them with nature. But we had a bigger plan for Earth Rebirth: we were going to get our entire school to recycle.

If we thought going through the steps of forming a school club meant dealing with bureaucracy, getting K–12 students, teachers, and parents not only to allow the gigantic brown Waste Management recycling bins to be placed behind the school, but actually to bring their cans, bottles, and newspapers required more than a little patience and perseverance. We went to meetings, presented to classes, made sure the bins would fit. I know it doesn't sound like a lot of fun for a sixteen-year-old, but I had never been so motivated in my life. All the energy I channeled into getting in trouble was now being channeled into scheduling students to work at the drop-off each morning. They even gave me the Civitan Award for community service at graduation, and the local TV news aired a profile of me they called "Rebel with a Cause."

After graduation I moved to Eugene, Oregon, where I got even more involved in the environmental movement as a college activist fighting for spotted owls and against clear-cutting forests. I also turned eighteen and immediately registered to vote. By getting involved in an issue as a teenager, I saw firsthand how politics worked. Whether it was convincing various constituents at my school to buy in to our recycling program or voting on a ballot measure to protect Oregon's old growth forests, I knew that to create change you had to participate. Voting was one more way I could make my voice heard on issues I cared about. Most importantly, I learned that even when I was too young to vote, I could still make a difference.

ANASTASIA GOODSTEIN is an award-winning blogger and often-quoted expert on American tweens, teens, and early twenty-somethings. Her blog, Ypulse.com, reaches a highly influential audience of agency, brand, and media executives as well as social marketers. Her book about teens and technology, *Totally Wired*, was published by St. Martin's Press in 2007. (Photo credit: Andrea Scher)

★ Adrian Grenier ★

My essay entitled
"A Couple of Ridiculous and Not-So-Ridiculous
Paragraphs on Voting
Designed to Make You Vote"

I feel like I'm back in school. I've been avoiding this stupid-ass essay on why you should vote for months. Someone wants me to condescend to you and tell you why you should vote. Vote 'cause you'll get a hot fudge sundae, okay? Is that what you want? Do you need a reward for voting 'cause you can't make an informed decision on your own? Do you need grown-ups telling you what to do? No, you don't! Everyone seems to think you can't make the right decision on your own. But voting is telling those people, "Don't tell me what to do!" Do you think the world seems corrupt and you'd rather take up arms in dissent? Me too!

But check this out: voting is the simplest form of rebellion against tyranny. Vote so you don't have to march in the streets in protest. That's a real pain in the ass. Vote because they're telling you what to do and *you* should be telling *them.* Vote because the powers that be don't want you to. They think you're young and dumb. They don't want to hear you stand up and say, "No, not you, the other guy." Why do you think they make such an effort to prevent you from voting? Why do you think they try to steal your vote? Why do you think they hold elections on a weekday, when everyone has to work or go to school? 'Cause it makes it harder to say, "I vote for the person who is not you, because you have been fucking everything up."

A lot of important and intelligent people tell us

to vote. So there must be something to it, right? They seem to think if we all vote, we can make a difference. Well, let's all vote and see if they're right! Or better yet, let's at least do it to prove them wrong. Less than 50 percent of registered voters actually vote; so what would happen if 100 percent voted? What would happen if more people registered? I just want to see what would happen if everyone voted. Just once. If everyone does and we elect a pathetic imbecile to the White House, then our cynical instincts will be proven right and all the smarty-pantses telling us to vote all the time will have to shut up. We can finally be satisfied that the voting process is in fact bullshit, and we can all sleep in on voting day, doubt-free. But until then, there will always be "what if we tried?"

The truth is I can't tell you why you should vote because I don't know you. Everyone is trying to get you to vote, but who has the authority? Not me! I'm just as cynical and jaded as you. I vote to rebel, sure, but I also vote because why the fuck not? I was apathetic the greater portion of my life. I never believed that my vote mattered. And then, in 2000, I saw the results of my lack of participation and I couldn't bitch about it, because I hadn't done anything to stop it. I am fed up with the small fraction of people who do vote and then choose the wrong MF. Let's vote for the right president. Do it. It will be way better than having a president who sucks and doesn't speak for you and me. Let's try and shake things up! Too many old white men are telling us what to do. Let's see what happens if we get a woman elected, or a black man, or a Native or Cuban American, or a person with a twin sibling. What happens if— gasp!—a third-party candidate gets elected?! Things might actually get better. This is your world. Make sure it's your president.

New York native **ADRIAN GRENIER** is best known for roles on the HBO series *Entourage* and in *The Devil Wears Prada*. He is an executive producer of the upcoming Planet Green show *The Green Life*, as well as a gifted documentary filmmaker and self-taught musician.

★ Hill Harper ★

Many people are under the illusion that one vote—one voice cannot make a difference. For better or worse, a single voice spoken loud enough has tremendous opportunity to create a momentum that shapes a nation and thus shapes the world. Voting is essential because it changes not only the individual who votes but the community, city, state, nation, and ultimately the world in which they vote. Voting is much more than the one ballot cast on any particular day. Voting represents *participation.*

Something happens psychologically when a person participates in a community-based process. That voter, that participant, gets filled with more pride because they intrinsically understand that their vote matters, and therefore, that they *matter*. Additionally, a clear message is sent to those who are in so-called power letting them know that they must be accountable to the individuals who are casting ballots. History shows us that voting is almost like dominoes. The more we participate and vote, the more the system of governance changes for the better. So ultimately, we are in a representative democracy that functions properly only IF WE VOTE. It's oh so simple, but not easy.

Why isn't it easy? Well, since there is a direct correlation between voter turnout and change, it stands to reason that the individuals who are in power at any given time have a disincentive to encourage people to vote and participate. The people in power want to convince you that you and your vote don't matter—because if they are successful in doing so, they know it increases the likelihood that they will remain in power. As weird and illogical as it may sound, the government is one of the main culprits of falsely convincing you that you and your vote don't count. They do that by spreading "FEAR"—which, for me, stands for "False Evidence Appearing Real." Many powerful government and corporate groups put out false evidence that appears real to convince you that your vote doesn't matter. Want examples? How about polling data? Most polls are sponsored by major multimillion-dollar companies and news and research organizations that all have lobbyists in Washington. They have deep-rooted big-money interests in controlling what you think. To that extent they can convince you through a "poll" that your candidate is "so far behind" in their poll that whether you vote or not will not effect the outcome of an election (i.e., "your vote doesn't count"). False Evidence Appearing Real!

So then, this begs the question of why does it seem that this so-called representative democracy hasn't been working effectively for the people. Why? Well, *the people* haven't been voting. That's you and me: *the people*. We, the people, by giving away our power and not participating by voting have effectively transferred all of our created power and influence to lobbyists and major corporations. Why vote? Well, we need to take the power back. The constituents that the lobbyists and the major corporations serve are not you and me. They are their corporate shareholders, and not just the mom-and-pop shareholders who trade stocks on E*TRADE. They are servicing the billionaire shareholders who look to increase their wealth by decreasing your power.

This is not a game. It is real life. And yes, you could choose like many are doing right now to shrink away from your life and live a smaller life than you were born to live. But I know the time has come for you to truly live your life in the grand magnitude that you deserve. And if you live fully and embrace your power, the reflective light you shine on the world will never be as bright as it should be; unless you vote. Choosing to vote makes you count. Stand up and be counted. Dream Big. Act Bigger. Shine and participate. Your vote is your voice. Voting is you. And you are voting. Now. Today. Every day. You vote. Reflect that. Embrace that. Live that. And shine. Shine with *your voice*! We need to hear it! Vote.

HILL HARPER is an actor, writer, and philanthropist. A graduate of Brown University, Harvard Law School, and Harvard's Kennedy School of Government, he founded the MANifest Your Destiny Foundation, which provides mentorships, scholarships, and grants to underserved young men. His many acting roles include his starring gig on *CSI: NY*, and he is the author of the award-winning, best-selling book *Letters to a Young Brother.*

★ RACHAEL HARRIS ★

REBECCA HARDING
FOR STUDENT COUNCIL SECRETARY

Let me tell you a story about what happened in my high school. Everyone who had a brain somehow "forgot" or "didn't have time to" or "was too baked to remember" the student council elections. And Rebecca Harding became secretary. Not even president. Just secretary. Of course the other officers were harmless kids, who only wanted the title for their college applications. But not Rebecca Harding. She was a conniving, power-hungry bitch who used her position to ruin life for everybody.

When we would gather for assemblies, Rebecca, "the monitor," as we called her, would stand up to address the school with "The Secretary's Announcements," as she called them, and the room would shudder. She would read the announcements as if she were giving orders to the Starship *Enterprise*, and it was under attack.

"The Spirit Assembly next Friday is mandatory. Repeat: MANDATORY.

"Submissions for prom theme received after last Thursday have been disqualified, as the deadline was clearly published in the student council minutes dated 3/10. As there were no QUALIFIED submissions for prom theme, the secretary has chosen the theme 'Chastity Rocks.' This decision is permanent."

If anyone snickered or whispered ANYTHING TO ANYONE while Rebecca was listening to the sound of her voice, which she loved, she would laser in on them and give them the scariest, steeliest shut-it-or-I-will-come-over-there-and-shut-it-for-you glare. If that didn't work, she'd pull out this old chestnut: "I'll wait." As if anyone didn't know that. And oh yes, she had the full support of the faculty, who lauded her as a "real go-getter" but who also were just as afraid of her as the students were.

One time, a teacher bumped into Rebecca in the lunch line and Rebecca had it classified as a federal hate crime because the teacher had a Lebanese pen pal.

Okay, that last one isn't true, but she had it all planned out in case it ever happened.

How do I know this?

Well, because Rebecca Harding was me. Get it? Rachael Harris. I know, clever.

Now I'm proud to report that after several thousand hours of therapy and a string of moderately critically acclaimed acting jobs, I'm not like that anymore. But you're fooling yourself if you think people like Rebecca Harding always loosen up after high school.

Most of them become politicians. A small handful become top chefs, but let's not focus on them. Most power-hungry insecure paranoid megalomaniacs go into politics. And they only ever get elected *when the cool kids don't vote.*

Occasionally some kid would come up to me in high school and say, "You think you're so important, but guess what? I didn't vote for you."

Know what I'd say? "Huh. Weird. Because guess what? I'm still running your life. And if you didn't vote, you can't complain. Lame-o!" And then I'd lay down a silent fiber-cereal fart and walk away.

So don't take this lightly. When the Rebecca Hardings of this world get into office, America gets a crappy prom theme. And by prom theme, I mean foreign policy, and by crappy, I mean war with no end. Or by prom theme, I mean food supply, and by crappy, I mean insane amounts of mercury. You get the idea. The stakes are high.

I hear you thinking—my hearing is as razor sharp as it was in high school. I hear you thinking, "But Rachael, you had like six hundred people in your high school. Of course one vote could make a difference there."

Well, what if I told you I had more than three hundred million people in my high school? Not buying it? Okay, let's try this: you're absolutely right. In this big country, one vote actually does not make a difference.

There. How about that? I totally just said that. But now I'm going to go one step further than anyone else in this book and say that's why voting alone is not enough. One vote does not make a difference, so that's why YOU HAVE TO DO MORE THAN VOTE.

But not that much more. I'm not saying you have to join a campaign or make phone calls or anything sucky. But what you have to do is this simple thing: you have to discuss the candidates and issues with your friends. Guess what? This is Rebecca Harding talking to you now. Discussing the candidates and issues with your friends IS MANDATORY.

That way, your one vote isn't just one vote. It becomes part of a trend. You influence people who respect your opinion, and you let them influence you as well. You start asking questions. "What do you think of this guy?" "Is he as crazy as he looks?" "What about this woman?" "I'm leaning toward the guy with the huge ears, and here's why." And my favorite, "What in God's name does this proposition mean?"

Voting isn't a requirement; it's a right. A right guaranteed to every American citizen by the Constitution. And while your single vote might not guarantee you the candidate of your choice, or a "pass" on a proposition, for that matter, it will undeniably guarantee you a little known right buried deep in the fine print of the Constitution . . . the right to bitch.

So the next time Rebecca Harding gets elected, you can say with conviction, "Congratulations, Rachael. You won. I didn't vote for you in this election, and I think you suck." Then you can lay your own fiber-cereal fart.

RACHAEL HARRIS is an actress and comedian. She is a member of the comedy troupe The Groundlings, and can currently be seen on the television show *Notes from the Underbelly*. She has also been a correspondent on *The Daily Show with Jon Stewart* and has appeared in many television shows and films, including VH1's *Best Week Ever*, *Fat Actress*, *Evan Almighty*, *Best in Show*, and *For Your Consideration*. Originally from Ohio, Rachael Harris now lives in Los Angeles.

★ MOLLY IVINS ★

Look at it this way. Voting whitens your teeth, sweetens your breath, and perks up your sex life. Voting is new and improved, stops the heartbreak of psoriasis, and improves your gas mileage. Voting makes you feel virtuous, is your patriotic duty, and entitles you, absolutely free, to four years of guilt-proof gritching about what's wrong with the country. Those who do not vote forfeit the right to complain.

Voting causes fat to disappear. Poof! Up to ten pounds gone in just one trip to the polling place.

Standing in the voting box improves your IQ, and enables you to think of witty responses *at the very moment* you need them. Besides, if you don't vote, it will all be your fault.

Voting is a friendly thing to do. You get to meet your neighbors. Also, romances have been known to start while standing in line to vote.

Voting prevents underarm stains, ring-around-the-collar, carpet odor, and dust bunnies. Exercising your franchise will firm and tone both your abs and your glutes. Using your suffrage takes weight off your thighs and makes you a more pleasant person all around. There are countless recorded cases of people whose personalities improved dramatically after voting.

Also, voting is the only way to make political ads go away.

And it cures acne.

Politics is not about *those people* in Washington or

those people at the state capitol. Politics is about us: you, me, and the guy next to us. *We* run this country, *we* own this country, and *we* have a responsibility to hire the right people to drive our bus for a while.

The three great excuses are: "Sorry, I'm just not interested in politics," "Oh, they're all crooks," "Well, there's nothing *I* can do about it."

Politics is not a picture on a wall or a television program you can decide you just don't care for. Our entire lives are set into and written by the warp and woof of politics.

Political decisions affect your life every day in thousands of ways. Whether the food you eat is safe, what books your children read in school, how deep you will be buried when you die, if the lady who dyes your hair is competent, how safe your money is in stocks or banks, whether you have a job, whether you have to go fight in a war, who is qualified to prescribe your eyeglasses—that's all politics.

No, they're not all crooks, and most of them go into politics out of idealism, whether you like their ideas or not. Sure, the system is corrupted—by money, the usual suspect. But it can be fixed, and whether it is fixed is also up to us. American politics has earned a heavy dose of cynicism from all of us, but the ideas behind our politics have not. It's our heritage, our political legacy, most of us get it free just for being born here:

> "We believe these truths to be self-
> evident, that all men [and women] are
> created equal, that they are endowed by
> their Creator with certain unalienable
> Rights, that among these are Life, Liberty
> and the pursuit of Happiness. . . . That
> whenever any Form of Government
> becomes destructive of these ends, it is
> the Right of the People to alter or to abolish
> it . . ."

After two hundred years, that statement is still so revolutionary, people all over the world are willing to die for it. They died in South Africa, they died at Tiananmen Square, and they died in Myanmar. A lot of Americans have died to preserve those ideas. Don't throw them away out of boredom or cynicism or inattention.

"There's nothing *I* can do about it." If the presidential election in 2000 didn't teach you that every vote counts, you may want to consider assisted living. Of course, you don't have as much say in this country as the people who give big money to the politicians—but that can be fixed. As an American living today, your one vote means you have more political power than 99 percent of all the people who ever lived on this planet. Think about it: Who ever had this much power? A peasant in ancient Egypt? A Roman slave? A medieval shoemaker? A French farmer? Your grandfather?

Why throw power away? Use it. Leverage it.

Besides, the election won't end unless you vote.

Only you can stop it.

This essay was originally published by newspapers all over the United States on November 2, 2004.

MOLLY IVINS was a newspaper columnist, political commentator, and author. She was raised in Texas, and known for her sharp wit and satire, combined with a colorful and creative language style, which others dubbed "Molly-isms." She died in 2007.

★ MIKE JAMES ★

Whether you vote or not depends a lot on what you saw when you were growing up. When I was a kid, my parents didn't vote. Why? Because *their* parents didn't vote, and so on and so on, back as far as I could see.

When you grow up in a household where it's not important to vote, you learn—you *believe*—that your vote doesn't count. Until recently, I believed that. It was like a curse that had been handed down for generations: your vote doesn't count. Which is just another way of saying *you* don't count.

Then, in 2004, I came to my senses. I voted, exercising a right that many African Americans had fought and paid dearly for: the chance to have their voices heard. That first time I voted, I felt very important. I felt, to the marrow of my bones, that my vote *did* count, *did* make a difference. That's why today my goal is to help more young adults understand the importance of going out and registering to vote. Every citizen in this country has a voice, and it's a voice that needs to be heard. If you don't vote, you really can't complain about who's in office because you had a chance to make a difference and you didn't take advantage of it.

By voting, I want to make a difference in my neighborhood, my state, and my country. One of the most effective ways I can make a change is by voting for the person I want to lead the city, the state, and the nation. Through the grace of God, I pray that I—and everyone who votes—will make the right decision and that we will elect someone to office who will make the right decisions for our country.

I already know the person I would like to vote for in the 2008 presidential election. I haven't chosen my candidate because of sex, ethnicity, or political party. My decision is based on who I believe will cause the most positive change in our country.

Sometimes it feels as if candidates want to win an election just to say they won "the game." However, democracy is not Monopoly; in fact, if you want to compare it to a board game, you'd have to say it's the game of Life, and that means that the stakes are very high. So my advice is don't judge who to vote for with your eyes. Use your ears. Listen to what the candidates say. Read what they stand for on their Web sites and in newspapers and magazines. Pay attention. Your vote will help determine the future of the United States of America.

Occasionally I think that Americans have become selfish. It seems that all anybody cares about is what they can do to make their own lives better. No one seems to be trying to help the next person, the person who may not be fortunate, famous, or influential. We need a leader who thinks about *all* people in every decision he or she makes, not just *some* people. That goes for international relations as well. Our country has lost a lot of respect around the world. It's up to us, the voters, to elect someone who will make decisions that will earn America the respect of other nations.

The only way our country can succeed is for

every citizen to go out and vote for the person he or she believes can make a positive change. So vote for the person you believe can make a difference. Just VOTE.

MIKE JAMES is a point guard for the New Orleans Hornets, and was the first undrafted player in NBA history to average at least twenty points a game in a season. He is also the founder of the Mike James Scholarship Foundation, which helps at-risk students from disenfranchised communities get financial assistance for college. James lives in Houston with his wife and four daughters.

★ MARTIN KAPLAN ★

I VOTED

I don't know her name. She's probably well into her seventies by now, and though she must have been nearly twenty years younger when I first saw her, I can't say that she looks any different today. You know the look: perfectly groomed, everything in place, classy, refined. The makeup, the jewelry, the clothes, the hair: you'd never notice any of it, because the whole idea is for it to seem effortlessly appropriate. I usually see her once a year, sometimes more, and I guess there've been some years when I haven't seen her at all. In my mind, I call her the Voting Lady, though I suppose the Polling Place Lady would be more accurate, because when I see her, she isn't voting, she's checking people in to vote at my polling place.

My polling place migrates, like Brigadoon. For years, when I first lived in the neighborhood, it was in a house around the corner from mine, right in the middle of a block of other houses, only this one had a big flag outside. I used to think it was her house. She sat at a table in the foyer, showing people where to sign next to their address in a big ledger book that she had, upside down, in front of her; the lady next to her would then hand me my ballot. When my kids were little, I always brought them with me, and the voting lady always said something supportive, like, "Never too young to teach them about America." Since at least one of them usually wanted to be carried, it wasn't easy for me to do that as well as work the stylus on the ballot at the same time, and when they were a little bigger, they enjoyed fighting over which of them would get to punch the holes, which reliably won me a hairy eyeball from the Voting Lady because, as she pleasantly but firmly reminded me, only registered voters are allowed to actually vote. I think it left my kids feeling not so much that the Voting Lady was mean, but that the privilege of the stylus was a power akin to wielding Excalibur.

Some years, my polling place was in the auditorium of an elementary school in the neighborhood, close enough so that I could walk there, too, and there she was again, which made me realize that the house on McCadden where I used to vote wasn't really her house at all, that she was a volunteer or maybe paid just a token fee for her efforts. When I approached the box with my completed ballot, she would tear off a perforated stub and give it to me as a receipt. I VOTED—HAVE YOU? it said. I was never sure what to do with it. Leave it along with a tip at lunch? Prop it on my dashboard? Magnet it to my refrigerator as a smug souvenir? She also always gave me a little oval sticker for my shirt: I VOTED, it said, on a field of stars and stripes. The sticker, more subtle with its subtext than the stub, was, I thought, more in keeping with her own understated elegance.

One year, when there seemed to be one election day a month because of a California gubernatorial recall vote and its aftermath, I stupidly failed to check the instructions on the sample ballot I got in the mail, and when I got to the elementary school on June Street, the only thing going on in the auditorium was a rehearsal of a Thanksgiving play. So I walked home, went online to find my polling place (I'd thrown the sample ballot away), drove to a high school I'd never noticed before, and there she was.

That year, for the first time, I wondered whether she was a poll-watcher not just because she cared about democracy but perhaps also to be around other people, make friends, maybe even meet a guy—there were always a number around in her age bracket, though rarely ones I thought well-turned-out enough to deserve her.

A couple of years, during presidential elections, my polling place was a Lutheran church on Melrose, with way too few on-street parking places set aside and huge lines snaking out the door onto the sidewalk, at least when I got there, which was half an hour before the polls opened. These were times when I really, really wanted to vote. It was better than screaming about how I felt, which I also wanted to do, and for once the idea of being in a long line actually pleased me, because it meant that there were lots of other people just as determined as I was to let their votes do their shouting for them. Once inside the church, I discovered that this polling place combined several different precincts' voters. A man at the door asked me my address and directed me to a green-covered table, where I was relieved to find, amid the throng and the confusion, my Voting Lady—not, like Ruth, in tears among the alien corn, but instead perfectly serene, going about her duties completely unruffled by the tumult and the cacophony, whose noise must have been to her the music of democracy.

The busiest, and oddest, election day I ever saw her, though, was when members of my newly constituted neighborhood council were chosen. If I told you how many candidates there were and how many times I could vote for each of them (depending on, for example, whether I owned a business in the neighborhood or belonged to various civic groups or where my kids were in school), and how many different desks I had to go to in order to collect the different parts of my ballot, and how long it took to complete the process, well, you probably wouldn't believe me. The polling place was a firehouse on Wilshire; the stakes involved zoning and historic preservation, and it was impressive how the rival neighborhood factions, between whom no love was lost, had turned out amazing numbers of their button-wearing supporters, most of whose faces didn't bother to conceal their self-righteousness or mutual contempt. Yet, in the midst of this, the unflappable politeness of the Voting Lady, seated at a card table a few feet from the firemen's bench press, seemed—to me, anyway—to acquiesce to the upside of the civic combat raging around her and to emanate reassurance that all would ultimately be resolved peacefully and democratically.

On the other hand, there was one election day when only a handful of county judgeships and seats on the local community college board were on the ballot. When I came in to vote, it was obvious that I was the only voter there. I wondered how I should play it with the Voting Lady. Commiserate about the sorry lack of commitment on the part of my fellow citizens? Say something encouraging about more people surely coming later? Blame it on the unsexiness of the races? But before I could decide what face to present to her, she threw me exactly the cue I needed. She greeted me as though there might have been scores of other voters around us, marking ballots in their booths. Even if there were not, her face and tone and beautiful posture announced to me that this election day, by its sheer existence, and this voter, me, merely by showing up, were all that was needed to manifest in all its full-ness the miracle of democracy, and to justify the blood spilled by generations past to make this day possible, and to make my rendezvous with it the most fortunate destiny on the face of the planet.

I may be making this up, but when she stuck the
I VOTED oval on my jacket, I could swear that she
winked at m

MARTIN KAPLAN is the Norman Lear Chair in Entertainment,
Media and Society at the University of Southern California's
Annenberg School for Communication, where he is the founding
director of the Norman Lear Center. Find out more at
www.learcenter.org.

★ SEAN KINGSTON ★

I feel honored to be a part of this *Declare Yourself* opportunity to talk about what voting means to me, and what it means as part of the bigger picture.

I write this just as a seventeen year old, but by the time the 2008 elections roll around, I'll be eighteen years old and able to vote. My first time voting!

My parents were born in Jamaica, but I feel so blessed to be American and have the chance to follow my dreams. Turning eighteen means I have earned the right to vote and my opinion has the right to be heard. Knowing that my parents did not have the same opportunities that I have now makes voting even more special. I think it's easy for people to take voting for granted when they do not know what it is like not to have the right to vote. It means so much to me to know that I have this privilege to make a difference!

They always stress to our age group to do the right thing—voting is the right thing! Only when I was asked to write this did I really begin to understand what the right to vote means for the country, and I wanted to share my thoughts in hopes of encouraging you to participate.

Voting is something you should want to do, and you should understand the candidates' platforms, beliefs, and plans—all of it—and figure out what their vision of the future is. I look forward to hearing what each candidate has to say. A lot of times we are asked to choose sides in life, and in this case it's not about sides; it's about deciding on the topics that are important to you.

As young people with huge futures ahead of us, it's good to start off on the right foot. We all face obstacles and events in life that we have to understand and make decisions about—it's no different with voting.

Voting is not just a right; it is a responsibility. Be inspired to vote and encourage your friends to do the same.

SEAN KINGSTON is a young musician who combines rap, reggae, pop, and doo-wop to create a unique new sound. Sean quickly became a household name with his number-one single "Beautiful Girls" and follow-up single "Me Love." He has performed on NBC's *Today*, ABC's *Jimmy Kimmel Live!*, BET's *106 & Park*, and MTV's *TRL*. You can visit him online at www.seankingston.com. (Photo credit: Mark Mann)

★ James Kotecki ★

The Cynical Revolution

Maybe the reason a lot of young people don't vote is not that they're inherently lazy or apathetic. Maybe many young people have taken a good hard look at what's out there, and they haven't found anyone worth voting for. I chalk that up to entrenched cynicism.

It's no surprise that my generation is very cynical of political news. We know about sound bites. We know about editing to take things out of context—we watch *The Daily Show*, after all. Every time we see a strange picture, we're likely to assume it's been Photoshopped. For many of us, our favorite political news moment was when Jon Stewart went on the now-canceled cable shout-fest *Crossfire* and asked Tucker Carlson and Paul Begala to stop hurting America. We all agreed with Stewart: the media is a rather warped prism for directing political thought.

We're even more cynical of politicians. We know about how they use the media to manipulate public opinion. Whenever we see politicians on television, we assume that they have paid high-powered media consultants to tell them how to speak and act in this distorted-reality environment. They know how to look into the camera and act like they care, and how to deliver carefully scripted sound bites and jokes in a way that sounds natural. When we see them on television rehashing the same talking points for the millionth time, we don't trust that we're hearing the full truth.

But most of all, we're cynical about the political process. The first major, memorable political event for our generation was the Monica Lewinsky scandal—not exactly a bipartisan lovefest. Our first major election was the 2000 recount debacle, when half the country felt disenfranchised, and the entire country—at least as it was portrayed on cable news—became even more deeply entrenched in partisan bickering.

And yet, we know that all of these partisan divisions do not in any way mirror the actual way that real human beings interact or think about politics or come to conclusions about issues—especially younger people who are tired of the traditional two-party divisions.

Combine a feeling of disgust for political news, distrust in politicians, and disbelief in our political process in the mind of a newly minted eighteen year old, and you get a very understandable result—cynicism that displays all the symptoms of apathy.

Here's the thing, though. Despite all of those valid criticisms, I still vote. Call me naive, but I still believe that the decisions that our leaders make are too big for them to make without our input on what those issues, and what those decisions, should be.

Plus, I'm kind of a political geek. A big one, actually.

I'm guessing that if you're reading this, you're planning to vote, too. Let's face it: if you were an apathetic non-voter who did for some reason pick up this book, would you read the entry by the political video blogger or the one by Tyra Banks? Thought so.

So now we've established two things: young people don't vote because they're cynical of the political process, but you and I do vote because we care.

But how do we convince the cynics in group A to join our voting party in group B?

Maybe we can start by not calling it a voting party—that sounds kind of lame.

I think there are two ways to convince people. One is to encourage our friends to vote. Good start, but rather limited in scope. Instead, why don't we work to change our political conversation so that our apathetic friends will actually feel connected to it, instead of cynical about it?

We, the active young voters, must convince our politicians, whether we're working on their campaigns, blogging about them, or just sending them an e-mail or comment on their videos, to abandon their CNN studio talking points and soaring platitudes and get real with us. The Internet makes it possible: anyone with a cheap webcam and a good message can talk to millions of people every day. What if a politician came to the places where we like to hang out, like YouTube, and just talked to us like regular people? What if they just video blogged to us every day without studio lights or makeup or communication consultants? Then, I think, our generation would think of politics as real again.

If politics becomes more about reality, our cynical generation will care more about it. Politicians are rooted in glossy media presentation styles that our generation has grown cynical of. They will not change on their own, but if pressured, and if encouraged when they do something positive, they just might.

Second, we can lead by example online. Since our generation understands the Internet better than any other voting block, small numbers of us can have a disproportionately large impact on politics. One person started the Facebook group "One Million Strong for Barack," a factor often mentioned in conjunction with Obama's success on the Internet. One young campaign worker, S. R. Sidarth, taped Senator George Allen's perceived racial slur against him and changed the balance of power in the Senate after the 2006 midterm elections. I interviewed seven presidential candidates for my YouTube channel—two of them from my college dorm room using a webcam—and I'm twenty-one years old.

Notice anything constant here? The Internet empowers young people like never before. Our generation uses the Internet to organize weekend parties and Facebook tributes to *The Office*. Now, those of us who are politically active can use it to have more individual impact on the political process than any previous generation could dream of. So while you're trying to convince politicians to be real, make yourself heard on the Internet as well. You might not swing an election, but take it from me: if you keep at it, and you use social networking to your advantage, you could prove to your friends how powerful one voice can be.

Let's break voter apathy by building up politicians who will be real with our media-cynical generation, and by showing our peers how much power we have when we leverage the Internet to fight for our causes. You say you want a revolution? Well, you know, we all want to change the world. But wanting is not the same as achieving. So let's get to it.

JAMES KOTECKI started his video blog from his college dorm room in January 2007 and has since interviewed seven presidential candidates, including John Edwards. He has appeared in major national and international media outlets, and he has covered the 2007 Iowa Straw Poll and the CNN/YouTube Democratic Debate. You can catch his daily video series, Playbook TV, on Politico.com.

★ NICOLE LAPIN ★

When Arnold Schwarzenegger became governor of California, I was living in Paris. I thought that no one there would care. Then, as I was walking into class that morning at the political university there, Sciences-Po, a handful of student journalists started asking me, *"Tu es Americaine*?!" I said in French, "Yes, why?" Immediately they turned on their handheld recorders to get my reaction to the California gubernatorial race before I could figure out that, yes, they did care.

A couple of years later, I was back in the States when student riots broke out in the suburbs of Paris, but I didn't think anyone at work would care. Then, I walked into my morning meeting and the news director at a local station I was working for in California asked me to do a story on the unrest in France. I was on the air before I could stop and realize, yes, they care.

Sure, I had doubts and bought into the clichés that we don't care for a second. But I am here to tell any current or future doubters: We aren't the apathetic generation that we've been called time and again. We are an active, motivated group of passionate young people. We care.

Young people are rocking the worlds of business, entertainment, and social activism. So, to prove it to everyone else, I started a series on CNN.com that features people under thirty doing amazing things: Young People Who Rock.

But, America, there's a problem. Eighty percent of young French turn their caring into voting.[1] Yet, only 47 percent of Americans 18–25 voted in 2004.[2] (Kudos for the 11 percent increase from 2000.)[3] *Mon Dieu!* That amounts to an *F* on this side of the pond; in France it's an *I*, or *insuffisant*. Germans would give us a *5*, or *ungenügend*. Wherever you are, it basically sucks.

I know, I know, we don't like the idea of failing. We're smart. Too smart to vote, huh?

I keep hearing from some of the smartest people I know: "The system is broken." "My vote won't count; it's like a drop in the ocean." "The candidates and campaigns don't contact me." "Voting doesn't affect my life personally." "No one gets me."

I get it. We're idealists. I know I am. We're dreamers. We want a perfect system, and it's clear to us that it doesn't exist.

Every day, I see improvements that can be made

when reporting on politics. Am I disillusioned by the shortfalls? Do I opt out of the system because of them? *Au contraire.* I'm inspired to keep playing my role in it.

I've declared myself a journalist, a reporter, a card-carrying member of the Fourth Estate. Historically my role refers to the capability to frame political issues of the three estates of *parlement.* It hasn't changed since the French Revolution, when the term came about, except to say that the issues and information I gather now come from a representative government.

What will you represent? Will you have a role in this system? How will you declare yourself?

Pollsters declare themselves. They find statistics like this one: 72 percent of Americans 55 and older voted in the last presidential election.[4] Numbers matter. Not many candidates or campaigns contact us because our numbers give them no incentive.

Lobbyists declare themselves. They look at the, gasp, numbers, and they find more work with the powerhouses like the American Association of Retired Persons, or AARP. Is there an American Association of *Young People?* No. No one gets us—that's why.

Legislators declare themselves. They listen to the special interests, whether we like it or not. That's in large part why we see a ton of money spent for specialized museums, horse trails, and bridges to nowhere. You're right: voting might not affect *your* life personally right now, but it can because it's affecting others.

Gators *didn't* declare themselves. That's right, Gators from the University of Florida. I'm not discriminating; University of Miami Hurricanes didn't declare themselves, either. Nor did enough college students in Florida in 2000. While we talk about those stinking numbers, how about this one: the number of votes that decided the election, 537. When those smart people not-so-smartly say that their vote doesn't matter, that it's a drop in the ocean, I ask them, "If more college students voted eight years ago, would our history be different?"

I don't have an answer to the gripe that the system is broken. We are in an imperfect system, and we're savvy enough to get that. With the same zeal that drives us to rock the professional world, though, we can get it fixed. We're also really lucky to have the opportunity and the time to see it fixed.

In China a failing grade is *cha*, 差; in Tunisia it's a *12*; in Egypt it's ضعيف جدًا. Young people in those countries can fail like the rest of us, but they can't fail at voting like we do. They can't vote.[5]

I report on those countries all the time, telling their stories, reporting their rough drafts of history. What's really exciting is that our generation's story hasn't yet been told. It hasn't even happened yet. When that time comes, I want to tell our story. So, give me something good to report, something that will shock, surprise, and inspire them all. Don't *just* care. Declare yourself.

NICOLE LAPIN is a news anchor at CNN. She created *Young People Who Rock*, a weekly profile series featuring people under thirty who are doing amazing things to change the world. Lapin graduated summa cum laude and as class valedictorian from Northwestern University's Medill School of Journalism, earning honors in her double major in political science. (Photo courtesy of Laura Grier)

[1] International IDEA Institute for Democracy and Electoral Assistance

[2] http://www.census.gov/population/www/socdemo/voting.html

[3] http://www.civicyouth.org/?page_id=241

[4] http://www.census.gov/population/www/socdemo/voting.html

[5] Freedom House (2007). "Freedom in the World 2006". Freedom House/Rowman & Littlefield. ISBN 0-7425-5802-9.

★ THOMAS LENNON ★

I suppose at this point in my life I am comfortable enough to confess something that until now I have kept secret from my closest friends, my wife, and family.

I'll get to that in a moment.

Let me begin by saying that to my knowledge, I have never voted for the winner of a presidential election. . . . Well, maybe one time. But considering that I've been voting since the eighties, and I've only picked one winner, you'd think I would be discouraged—but I'm not. If I cared so much about winning, why would I play blackjack all the time? Maybe I should have quit that a few thousand dollars ago?

Actually now that I write that down, maybe I should have quit blackjack.

Anyway, I guess that's how I feel about voting. Despite the fact that I have almost never had to stay up late to watch some overrated "victory" party, I still vote, and I always will. Because I can. And the process is what it's all about. The thrill of doing it means more than the victory or the defeat. (At least I *think* so; you might have to ask a victor.)

And now, for the secret I've never told anyone:

I VOTED FOR ROSS PEROT.

American, Patriot, Musical-Theater Enthusiast, Thomas Lennon.

THOMAS LENNON is an actor, comedian, writer, and producer. He is the cocreator, along with frequent collaborator Ben Garant, of the television show *Reno 911*, on which he plays the role of Lieutenant Jim Dangle. The pair have cowritten screenplays for many hit films. Thomas Lennon got his start with The State, a comedy troupe that had its own show on MTV.

★ MAROON 5 ★

ADAM LEVINE

I don't trust politics. And I have very little faith in our political system right now. It saddens me to have come to that conclusion at the ripe old age of twenty-eight. I'm sure the last eight years and our numerous impeachable offenses against the world have something to do with it. And so does the fact that many Americans seem to have basically forgotten that Al Gore won the popular vote and was ELECTED. It's funny, but whenever I hear about conspiracy theories or accusations against people in our government, I'm literally never surprised. I definitely feel hardened to a certain degree. Which, come to think of it, isn't necessarily bad if you believe in that whole "things need to get worse before they can get better" theory. The most urgent issue, as far as I'm concerned, is repairing our global reputation. I find myself traveling all over the planet and apologizing for this mess! The idea of ignoring the world at large truly terrifies me. We need a hero in a big way. I despise politics, but I really love people. Let's find some who can turn this ship around.

MATT FLYNN

Asking people to agree on a presidential candidate is like asking people to agree on a restaurant. Somehow you always end up with pizza.

MICKEY MADDEN

Looking at the field of candidates in 2008, one

can't help feeling a creeping despair, if not a full-blown hopelessness. We are dealing with an embarrassment of poverties; never before has the discourse regarding the presidential election been so degraded and downright stupid. On the left, inasmuch as there is a difference between "left" and "right" in this age, we find such a desperate clamoring for change that we've elevated an entirely incompetent bunch of double-speaking political insiders to the level of potential saviors. Meanwhile, the right is consumed with its ugly and archaic identity politics, all the while candy-coating an utterly disastrous war that has left our economy, our reputation, and the country of Iraq in shambles in its wake; not to mention the scores of unnecessary dead for whom the idiots who authorized this war (on the left and on the right) would hopefully feel responsible. In the haze of our domestic "debate," I can barely recall one specific and/or pragmatic idea from any single candidate that would address the issues of poverty, gas prices, clean and efficient energy, the value of the dollar, the tragic destruction of New Orleans, or any other pressing concern shared by most Americans. Nor has the foreign policy "debate" touched on the Sudan, China, Russia, or South America, and it has barely alighted on Pakistan. All the talk of Iraq seems to be a vague bunch of "stay the course" drivel from the right and "get out as soon as possible" dreck from the left, which essentially amounts to the same point of view, one borne out of a total mystification as to how to actually deal with the war and its potential aftermath. The outrageous fear-mongering and unfounded panic regarding Iran seems to be the only other "issue" that occasionally warrants commentary.

Our system is ailing. It may in fact be completely dead. We are at the mercy of two parties that continue to inch more and more toward each other ideologically in all the ways that actually matter, all the while mounting a "culture wars" dog-and-pony show, showcasing conflicts of far less consequence than the real and pressing issues. Such conflicts serve to give voters the illusion that they have a choice, that Republicans and Democrats are as different as black and white, when in fact the political spectrum in America has become a distinct and dull gray.

It is the gray of private interest. We have completely sold our political parties to the highest bidders. Corporate business has no political affiliation. It seeks out power and feeds off of it, and it exists to make money, pure and simple. The executive branch has become a tool of lobbyists and CEOs, who not only manipulate and pressure candidates into fulfilling their will, but indeed pick and groom candidates from a very early stage so as to reduce the need for such manipulation and pressure down the road.

Capitalism simply does not work, at least not in the best interests of the many. The Great Depression proved this, and the lesson learned from the economic recovery of the forties and fifties is that capitalism can only be maintained by constant war and confusion. This is the world in which we live.

I offer no easy solution to such a bleak state of affairs, but I imagine that a total paradigm shift, in other words a revolution, is the only way to reverse our rapid decline. Our world, however, has become so enchanted by entertainment and simple, shallow pleasure that real freedom, and a deeper happiness than simple material comfort could ever provide, seems a more and more distant notion each day. This is the lull of capitalism. No less an American icon than Thomas Jefferson knew, in his own lifetime, that the republic was falling victim to the same patterns and decadences of the imperialists that it overthrew. He, that greatest of Americans, knew that revolution and rebellion were essential acts of patriotism, and entirely necessary in times of stagnation and oppression.

Voting, at the moment, is a mere gesture, and perhaps an important one. For any real change to come about, however, for any real whiff of freedom to waft through the air, the average American needs to make everyday life a political act, to exercise the freedoms that we are promised but denied, and to demand much more of ourselves: more happiness, more pleasure, more self-sufficiency, more liberty.

JAMES VALENTINE

I do it for the sticker. I don't take it off all day.

I love to announce to everyone that I fulfilled my civic duty by going over to my neighbor's weird garage, closing the curtain, and choosing the candidates that I feel can best represent me. (Actually I really like going over to check out my neighbor's garage; it's like going to an open house, except it's just the garage. So, I guess it would be like going to an open garage.)

Maybe if we appeal to people's vanities, they'll get involved. That sticker is what it's all about. It's on all the runways this season, and all of the starlets out here in Hollywood wouldn't be caught dead without it. If you are not wearing *that* sticker on *that* Tuesday, then forget about it. You're over.

Okay, maybe this is the wrong approach.

Why should people vote?

Voting is more important now than ever. Why? Special corporate interests have hijacked the democratic process. They seem to be among the very few that care these days. They are very well represented, channeling untold fortunes into pushing their agendas. They want all of the stickers to themselves. What about the rest of the country?

It's no wonder people are disillusioned. The democratic process doesn't seem to really affect our daily lives. However, you don't need to look far to see there are things that need to change, things that are affecting us profoundly. Health care, education, our environment, just to name a few. The special interests who have hijacked the process don't want you to care. Fortunately, with a little bit of attention from a lot of people, we can guide our government to look out for all of us.

So go vote. It's fun. Get the sticker.

JESSE CARMICHAEL

I'm about to consult the Universal Tarot of Marseille to come up with something to say about the current political climate. . . . I'm going to draw one card at random out of the deck. . . . It is the Four of Wands.

The suite of Wands refers to "Creating, Growing, Building." The Four refers to the concepts of "Making it Happen, Your Efforts Result in Concrete Manifestation, Initial Success."

I'm taking this to mean that we all have a hand in shaping the future we're gonna be sharing. We've had some good ups and some bad downs . . . and here we are now. Sometimes life is fun, sometimes it feels just about too difficult. And no one knows why we're here or exactly what we're all supposed to be doing. I don't think people get enough encouragement to follow their bliss, as Joseph Conrad recommended. And it seems a shame that people have to struggle to make ends meet doing something they don't want to be doing, without much meaningful reward. It's all about teamwork. I think we should deconstruct our societies . . . look at what's really serving us and what is a waste of our energies. Let's start over, from the basics up . . . we need Food,

Water, Shelter, Sanitation, Education, Creativity, Ethics. . . . *Hmmm* . . . here's where it gets tricky, 'cause that's somewhat of a personal matter . . . although I'd hope we could all agree on no murder or violence, and a healthy degree of respect for everyone around us. What about the distribution of wealth . . . ? How can we fix that? To be honest, just thinking about all these things makes me feel weak and guilty and sad. . . . I want someone else to come up with a solution, and then I'll be there to help. Maybe that's what everyone wants . . . even the politicians. . . . Maybe I'll have some more energy someday to really do something about what I'm talking about. Until then I will vote for whoever I think will do the most good for the most people. And hope that the senators and representatives really listen when people call in to voice their opinions. Anyone else got any better ideas?

MAROON 5 is comprised of Adam Levine, Jesse Carmichael, Mickey Madden, James Valentine, and Matt Flynn. Adam, Jesse, and Mickey first started playing together as a band in junior high. Their band's composition and their musical style evolved over the years, ultimately leading to James and Matt joining the group now known as Maroon 5. They have released two chart-topping albums, *Songs About Jane* and *It Won't Be Soon Before Long,* and have won two Grammys.

★ COURTNEY E. MARTIN ★

HALF THE COUNTRY'S POTENTIAL

I sat cross-legged on the floor with a half dozen teenage girls who were munching on baby carrots tentatively and playing with one another's hair. One rotated the tip of her finger around the smooth plastic of an iPod. Another texted her boyfriend. The smell of Victoria's Secret body lotion—pungent, fruity, adolescent—was in the air.

"So why do you think there is this huge pressure to be so thin?" I asked. I was interviewing them as part of my research for a book I was working on about perfectionism and body hatred among young women. These Manhattan princesses from Park Avenue turned out to be quite the anecdotal gold mine.

"It just feels like to be thin is to be worthy," one girl said. Her auburn hair lay against the bright blue of her tight Knicks T-shirt.

"Yeah, and if you can deprive yourself, if you can have that much self-control, it's like you've proven something," said another, her Tiffany bracelet lying limp on her tiny wrist.

Fast forward to that evening. I'm teaching Introduction to Gender Studies at Hunter College. Though I am just ten blocks from where I interviewed the anxious circle of Park Avenue teens, I am a world away. Hunter is a city school largely populated by working-class students, many of them the first in their families to go to college, a majority of them from an ethnic background other than that vaguest of catchall categories, white.

After taking attendance and frowning at one of the stragglers for being late again, this time with nachos and a Red Bull in hand, I introduce the day's topic.

"Today we are going to go back in time and look at the first wave of feminism: the suffragettes."

The students' eyes glaze over. A couple of the more vocal ones groan. They have come here from their corporate cubicle jobs as someone's assistant and their service jobs as someones's cook, maid, personal trainer. They are exhausted and thinking only about the future—their long train rides home, their warm beds, their American dream.

"Now, come on. Hang in there with me. I've brought a video clip." With this announcement they perk up. "Has anybody seen *Iron Jawed Angels*?"

A couple of errant hands fly up, but the majority shake their heads no.

"It is about the movement to get women the right to vote, which actually started all the way back in 1848, when Elizabeth Cady Stanton held a meeting of women in Seneca Falls, New York, and presented her 'Declaration of Sentiments,'" I explain. "It read, in part:

'We hold these truths to be self-evident: that all men and women are created equal; that they are endowed by their Creator with certain inalienable Rights; that among these are Life, Liberty, and the pursuit of Happiness; that to secure these rights governments are instituted, deriving their just powers from the consent of the governed.'

"What does that sound like?"

One of my favorite students, a young man with Asperger's syndrome and a wonderful sense of humor, shouted out, "The Declaration of Independence!"

"Right," I went on. "She modeled it after that. Okay, so that was in 1848. Does anyone know what year women finally got the right to vote in the U.S.?"

"Ah, was it 1900, miss?" a Haitian woman with tiny braids in her hair asked in a timid voice. She was the best writer in the class, though she was too modest to realize it.

"No, but good guess. Any others?"

Students from all over the room threw out numbers: "1940!" "1915!" "1920!"

"There it is! 1920!" I shout over their shouting. "Think about how long that took the next time you feel impatient for social change. Seventy-two long years."

"Whoa!" yelled out one of the most animated students, a nineteen-year-old Puerto Rican–American from a very conservative Catholic family. Her father was none too pleased with some of the lessons she brought home from my class, in which, of course, I took not-so-secret pride.

"Yeah, it was a long fight . . . which is why we need to remember it and be grateful for it. I'm going to show you a clip now," I explain. "This scene comes fairly late in the movie. Alice Paul, who was one of the leaders of the movement, has been imprisoned for protesting on the White House steps."

I dim the lights and my students' eager faces disappear into darkness. I press PLAY and slide into an empty desk as Hilary Swank, who plays Alice Paul so fiercely in the film, comes onto the screen.

Alice Paul is escorted by guards into the prison cafeteria. She is sat down at the end of a long row of female prisoners in front of a plate of standard food: meat, potatoes, bread. She takes one look and then pushes it away with her hand. The sound of the metal plate scraping across the wooden table is a sign to the other imprisoned suffragettes. They too push their plates away in a resounding chorus of solidarity. They begin to sing.

The next scene shows Alice being force-fed. Shrunken to skin and bones, she seems to swim in her drab prison dress as the two men in white suits throw her into a metal chair. They secure her arms and forehead with ominous, black leather straps and then stick a metal contraption in her mouth, forcing it open. Her eyes open wide and she coughs violently as they stuff plastic tubing in her throat and pour whisked eggs down it.

As I watch this scene, I immediately think about my interviews earlier in the day. The Manhattan princesses, just eight decades after getting the vote, are starving themselves again. They push their plates away, just as Alice Paul and Lucy Burns and

Emily Leighton did, but they are in penthouse apartments, not prison cafeterias. They are pushing away their fullest lives, not stagnation and inequality. They are probably totally ignorant of the legacy in which they starve.

When I press STOP and turn the lights back on, I am greeted by a sea of somber faces. One of my few white students, from Staten Island, breaks the silence. "That was harsh. Did that seriously happen?"

"Yes, absolutely. Hunger strikes were an important part of what actually got women the right to vote," I affirm. "The nineteenth amendment, ratified on August eighteen, 1920, reads, 'The right of citizens of the United States to vote shall not be denied or abridged by the United States or by any State on account of sex.' Makes you feel pretty grateful, doesn't it?"

"Yeah, super grateful," says a beautiful Ecuadorian

immigrant I had convinced to quit her job in a women's clothing boutique in the Bronx that was both underpaying and sexually harassing her. "And it is so weird to think that there are all these girls now who are anorexic and stuff, but for what?"

"I was thinking that exact same thing," I tell her. "These women were starving themselves in pursuit of equality and rights, and women today are starving themselves, it almost seems, as a way of shying away from those rights. As if we've finally achieved what we wanted and now we are scared to be our fullest selves."

I followed some of the students' gazes up to the clock and realized it was time to let them go. "All right, more next time. Thanks, everybody," I told them as they were already zipping up bags and heading for the door.

My Ecuadorian student lingered after. "Professor, can I borrow that movie?" she asked.

"Of course," I said, handing it over.

"It really got me thinking, like my mind is spinning, you know?"

"That's good. What are you thinking?" I ask, always gratified when a student is fired up at the end of one of my classes.

"I just realize that I can't take so much for granted. I owe so many people so much. Like, my mom worked in all these terrible jobs and left her family so that I could come to this country. And Alice Paul went through that so I could vote."

"Right, right," I say, nodding my head eagerly. "You are part of these amazing legacies that you can't forget."

"I gotta respect myself and my body. Do like you said and demand to be treated fairly at my job."

"And?"

"And what?"

"And vote, girl, you got to vote."

"Right, that too. Thanks, professor. This was really cool."

And with that, she stuffed the DVD in her giant Coach purse and walked out. I sat on the edge of the desk and took a breath as the sun set over the Manhattan skyline out the picture windows.

I had sometimes wondered, as I took on the project of researching and writing my book, if my priorities were in the right place. How could I focus on food and fitness obsession when my country was at war? How could I spend all this time researching eating disorders when there were people in Sudan struggling to survive a genocide where water, much less food, is scarce?

But my day of serendipitous New York interactions reminded me how connected everything and everyone are. As long as women—especially those who are young and idealistic—don't feel confident enough to step into their true power, take up space, make their voices and their votes heard, the world will continue to spin out of control. Women have an important, distinct contribution to make in the political process—not just voting, but running for office, influencing public debate, demanding more humane, compassionate methods of governance. Without them, without a sense of our fierce feminist legacy, America realizes only half of its wild, borderless potential.

COURTNEY E. MARTIN is the author of *Perfect Girls, Starving Daughters: The Frightening New Normalcy of Hating Your Body*. You can read more about her work at www.courtneyemartin.com. She has never voted for a presidential candidate that has won, but she still thinks it is important. (Photo credit: Nikolai Johnson)

★ MEGAN McCAFFERTY ★

EARNING THE RIGHT TO GRIPE
OR: HOW AN APATHETIC COLLEGE STUDENT
TURNED INTO AN ACTIVIST
IN JUST ONE ESSAY

Since this is the week before the election, one might assume that I'm obligated to "get political" to keep with this week's theme. I have to admit that I have intentionally avoided any political theorizing up to this point for two very important reasons: 1.) There's already an overabundance of columnists offering their opinions, and I firmly believe that too many chefs blow up the kitchen, and 2.) Political columns bore the bejeezus out of me.

That's just it. I'm not a "political" person. I'll be

the first to admit that, before this presidential election, I was politically pathetic. I was the type who'd get P.O.'ed when a presidential address would pre-empt all programming but a *Who's the Boss?* rerun. There is no name for the lowest level of apathy that makes a person resort to watching a *Who's the Boss?* rerun. But it's precisely this type of indifference that has annoyed me enough to write this column.

This is the first presidential election in which I am old enough to participate. (Remember the two big rewards for turning eighteen in the U.S.: voting and getting thrown in jail.) Despite my ignorance and lack of interest in the past, I have made it an obligation to find out about the candidates and their views in order to figure out for myself, who, if anyone, can run this country. I want to make sure that the candidate who gets my vote is the one that I want to vote for and not the one my parents or my friends have brainwashed me into thinking is right for the job. I'm not getting all flag-wavy here, but I think that as a U.S. citizen, it just makes *sense* to become involved in such an important election.

The assumption that such involvement would make sense to everyone my age was a dunderheaded error on my part. Now that I've educated myself on the issues, I've been accused of being a "groupie" (of the political kind, not the slutty backstage kind). I overheard a girl passing by my room the other afternoon, criticizing my decision to tape a poster on my door in support of my chosen political party. According to the passerby in the hall, putting up that poster meant I was "jumping on the bandwagon" and that it was hypocritical for me to suddenly support a candidate or a cause "just because there's an election."

Too frightened to fling open my door to find out who had uttered this incredibly IDIOTIC lapse of logic, I was left to ponder the following question: *When the hell else would I put a campaign poster on my door, if not during an election?* Doing it at any other time would be like betting on a Monday Night Football game in May.

Perhaps this naysayer has become embittered by the growing number of oh-so-cool COEDS OF CAUSES. Unlike those who feel genuinely passionate about an issue, they are the partakers and purveyors of pamphlets and posters who have turned social and political awareness into something trendy. It's political activism as fashion statement. And they wear their buttons and wave their banners with enthusiasm that grows proportionally with the amount of attention attracted by their actions. I am not one of those people. There is a huge difference between this fashionable facade and privately taping a poster to my door.

But it's not just about a piece of cardboard. It bothers me to think that someone would label me a hypocrite just because I've invested time and energy in thinking about the future of our country. Would I be better off if I were one of the girls I ate dinner with recently who hadn't even bothered to *register* to vote because they "don't know who to vote for"? When I asked if they had done any research to find out what the candidates stood for, they just looked at me blankly before mumbling something about "not having enough time."

There seem to be too many people who don't have enough time. A lot of students say they aren't voting in this election because they can't find a suitable candidate, yet they'll complain about what a mess our country is in right now. As far as I'm concerned, anyone who can't take the time to get informed and get in the voting booth doesn't have the right to take up anyone else's time complaining.

This column was published in my campus newspaper on Thursday, October 29, 1992. I was nineteen years old, a sophomore in college. A lot has changed since then, but the opinions expressed in this editorial remain the same.

MEGAN McCAFFERTY is the *New York Times*-bestselling author of *Fourth Comings, Charmed Thirds, Second Helpings,* and *Sloppy Firsts*. The Jessica Darling series has won honors from the American Library Association and the New York Public Library, and has been translated into ten languages, including Japanese, Turkish, and Hungarian. For more information, visit meganmccafferty.com. (Photo credit: Jerry Bauer)

★ NAOMI SHIHAB NYE ★

MAKING ARISTOTLE PROUD

*"We become what we are, as persons, by the
decisions that we ourselves make."*
—Aristotle

We warm up for voting all sorts of ways,

selecting favorite toys from toy baskets,

pointing at baked potatoes in cafeteria lines

instead of fries, staring at glossy advertisements

in catalogs imagining what we would pick

if we could pick one thing from each page.

I vote for the sandals without rhinestones, thank you.

We warm up for voting by listening deeply

to the words of candidates but also words

between the words and around the words

and silences after the words, timing and tones

in which the words are spoken. Possibly people listen

too much to what others say ABOUT the candidates

but this is also interesting listening

and we have to do it too.

Puffed-up words and solid ones mix and mingle.

We weigh one thing against another, saying

Probably not,

or *Maybe*, then *Yes*,

carrying lines and promises in our pockets,

pulling them out, staring at them,

asking ourselves what feels true.

It's a beautiful thing,

warming up for voting,

an education of its own kind.

It helps make us a real citizen

of the United States.

★　★　★

Not voting if one is voting age?

People should be fined, like in Australia.

Not a huge amount, but a kick in the pants.

I know someone who didn't vote because it rained.

I know someone else who wanted to catch a bite

before a movie so he bypassed voting.

Not voting is like being given a fabulous gift

And saying *Never mind,*

Too much trouble to take the wrapping paper off.

Personally I favor early voting

so I don't have to worry about breaking my leg

on voting day and not getting there.

Don't worry about the people who say

their candidate always loses.

You will meet them everywhere.

★　★　★

You will meet the people who don't vote

because their brother's vote cancels their own vote.

You will meet the person who only wears blue shirts

　　on voting day.

You will meet the woman who votes

for names she remembers from grade school

but knows nothing about any candidate.

She would never vote for a Rogelio because

she knew one once who lied.

Do something extra for voting.

Help elders who recently moved to assisted living

get registered again.

Stand somewhere holding a sign.

Even if half the people hiss at you. Smile back.

Wear a T-shirt made by a celebrity or make your own.

Go door to door.

★　★　★

Last time I went door to door for a local candidate

more than two-thirds of people in a nice

   neighborhood

said they never vote because elections are "fixed."

Or, "it doesn't matter." Or, "sorry, never take the

   time."

They acted proud of not voting.

I wanted to tell them they are insulting soldiers

who fight so people in other countries can vote

(which also seems strange to me).

Do people take voting for granted

just because they live in the United States?

What would Susan B. Anthony say?

A few years ago I worked on election day

in a humble neighborhood,

offering to drive elderly people

to the voting place.

One lady went in her bathrobe.

One lady, age 100, said, "Honey, thanks.

My son's coming to take me later.

But you know what?

I feel so strongly about voting,

if I didn't have anyone to take me

and someone showed up at the door

to rob and shoot me today, I'd say, *'Okay buddy,*

but you have to drive me by the voting place first.'"

NAOMI SHIHAB NYE is a poet, essayist, and novelist. She has received a Lannan Fellowship, a Guggenheim Fellowship, and four Pushcart Prizes. Her collection *19 Varieties of Gazelle: Poems of the Middle East* was a finalist for the National Book Award. Naomi Shihab Nye describes herself as "a wandering poet." She calls San Antonio, Texas, home. (Photo credit: Michael Nye)

HUGE DEMOCRACY GEEK
EVEN VOTES IN PRIMARIES

NASHUA, NH—Politically engaged citizen David Haas, 25, described by friends and acquaintances as a "big democracy geek," even votes in primaries.

"I can understand voting in the big elections, like for president or governor, or maybe even senator," longtime friend Gregg Becher said Monday. "But David votes in, like, mayoral and county-supervisor elections. How dorky is that?"

The right to vote, as guaranteed in the

Constitution, is among the hallmarks of the American democratic system. But Haas has exercised his franchise rights to an embarrassing extreme, voting in every federal, state, and local election since turning eighteen.

"Normally, David's a reliable, punctual employee," said Dorothy Raubel, owner of Raubel Garden Center, where Haas has worked for the past seven years. "But then there's that occasional Tuesday morning in April or November when he calls in saying he'll be late to work. It's a strange habit, but we've all grown accustomed to it by now."

Haas prides himself on being an informed voter, making sure to familiarize himself with candidates' positions before casting a vote. A self-described "independent" who tends to favor Democratic candidates, he can summarize the basic position of both major parties on most issues. As a result, Haas has endured the mockery and derision of those around him.

"On September tenth, he showed up late to work, and you could just tell he'd been voting," coworker Mike Summers said. "He was holding something in his hand, and we were like, 'Hey, Haasenpfeffer, whatcha got there?' He said it was the League of Women Voters candidate guide. So Rob [Mularkey] says, 'League of Women Voters? Now I know why you vote so much—you want to horn in on that hot women-voter action!' David didn't even smile; he just got all huffy and said the guide was from the morning paper and that copies were available to the public."

Richard Prohaska, Haas's next-door neighbor, can attest to Haas's strange dedication to the American political process. Over the years, Prohaska said he has seen him get into numerous doorstep discussions with campaign workers and canvassing local politicians.

"About two months ago, some alderwoman who

was up for reelection was going door-to-door pass-ing out leaflets," Prohaska said. "I took one, thanked her, and closed the door as fast as I could. About thirty minutes later, I'm backing the car out of the garage to wash it, and there's David talking to her on his porch. I go to get the hose, and when I come back, he's actually inviting her into his home. I was half-done waxing when she finally came out. Either they had one hell of a quickie, or David cares deeply about local politics. Knowing him, it was definitely the latter."

Though it's not clear why Haas insists on voting in every election, there is no shortage of speculation.

"My guess is, it's his way of hiding from the real world," said Jennifer Thorsten, Haas's sister. "He's always been interested in politics. He was on the debate team in high school and got a BA in poli sci in college. I've tried to get him to skip an election, but he never does. He says that only by exercising our democratic freedoms do we keep our democracy healthy and vital. Whatever, David."

This piece was originally published by *The Onion* on October 2, 2002, in Issue 38 • 36

THE ONION, "America's Finest News Source," is an award-winning publication and website offering its seven million readers—in print and online at www.theonion.com—a unique picture of the world they can't get anywhere else. *The Onion's* attention-grabbing headli .:s and photojournalism make it by far the most popular news organization in its class.

★ HAYDEN PANETTIERE ★

When I turned eighteen this past year, my first stop that morning was to the Declare Yourself office in Los Angeles to register to vote. It only took a couple of minutes to fill out the form on my laptop. But the feeling of going through a special rite of passage stayed with me all day—I could actually vote and exercise my right to pick who's running the country.

Many of my friends and peers think of getting their driver's license or taking their first drink as their big rites of passage. People need to know, though, just how powerful and important it is to vote for the first time. It's not just your vote that matters, but your vote when it is counted along with all the other votes cast by young people around the country.

You may not know it, but we are the fastest growing group of voters. It's a big group, getting bigger every day. Did you know that four million Americans turn eighteen every year? The people in Washington will have no choice but to listen to us—but only if we speak up; only if we exercise our voting rights and don't silence ourselves.

When many of my peers think of voting, they think of their parents going to the local polling place. Or they think of the presidential election as something that just happens to older people. I'm not sure they realize that who runs our country really does affect our lives just as much as it affects the lives of our parents and the older generation.

Eighteen to me means the right to vote—the right to have an opinion on who runs the country, on the wars we are involved in, on the environment, and on other issues affecting us at the moment. It's no secret that I feel especially strongly about protecting our endangered wildlife. It's a complicated international issue that won't get any better without leadership from Washington. When I go alone into the voting booth, the environment and endangered wildlife will be at the top of my mind. What will be at the top of yours?

I feel empowered by being eighteen, by being able to call myself an adult—finally! I encourage the youth of America—plus everyone older and younger—to get out there and voice your opinions at the polls in 2008 and beyond.

HAYDEN PANETTIERE is an actor and singer best known for playing the role of "Claire" in the television series *Heroes*. She began modeling at the age of five months and has appeared in several films. She is also active in many charitable causes. Hayden is originally from Palisades, New York, and now lives in Los Angeles, California. (Photo © Ursula Dureren/dpa/Corbis)

★ AMY RICHARDS ★

WHY VOTE?

The first time I voted I was in the fourth grade.
My elementary school did a mock election and I
was the only kid out of five hundred or so to vote
for independent John Anderson. I was slightly
embarrassed for losing in such a big way and for
possibly revealing a family secret—we were liberal—but I wasn't deterred. The next time I voted
it was official: I was eighteen and I proudly went to
my town hall and voted for Michael Dukakis.

I seem to have a knack for supporting only

losers, but outcomes aside, since that day in 1980, I have taken great pride in voting.

Voting is the one moment when I matter as much as the next person. Some people might be more powerful than me (say, Michael Bloomberg), richer (say, Bill Gates), more popular (say, Madonna), but this very act of voting is something we all can do and where no one gets bumped to first class. Though you might be able to buy your way onto the ballot, you can't (yet) buy your way into the voting booth. The process—though frustrating and certainly less accessible for some people—is intrinsically democratic.

I also love that voting takes place in schools and nursing homes and storage facilities; it keeps it local, which is what all politics should be, anyway, and sometimes forces us to come face to face with elements of our communities we might otherwise ignore or overlook or honestly just might not know exist. Accessing this one right might put us in situations we don't always want to be in—for instance, having to wait in line just like everyone else or having to witness firsthand how public schools are truly deteriorating. The process alone has the ability to humble some of us, even for a moment.

As someone who has made her career arguing for equality, I also value voting because it's an example of how the rest of society should be organized. No preferential treatment, no price tag, no accredited degree necessary. The only discrimination is based on age.

Though to be fair, in all of my excitement for voting, I also recognize that there is a big gap between the idea of voting and the reality of realizing this democratic value. One of my first activist endeavors was a cross-country voter registration drive where I witnessed the obstacles in just registering to vote.

One eighty-year-old woman told me she was too old to vote; another person claimed that a long-ago felony charge prevented him from voting; and a Mexican woman assumed that because she wasn't born in the United States she couldn't vote here, though she was a U.S. citizen. All of these myths persist because some people honestly prefer to limit access to voting.

When it comes to actually voting, there are even more hurdles, such as language barriers, limited hours, or just not enough energy to fight through a system that is riddled with minor errors, such as misspelled names or bad addresses. Of course, it doesn't have to be this way and some states are changing course. Oregon, for instance, has the highest voter turnout rate simply because all voters mail in their ballots—thus allowing them to do it on their own time. Other states, such as Minnesota, allow same-day registration, meaning you don't have to register thirty days before you vote, a fact not many people know, which gives them a higher turnout rate. The obstacles are problematic because what it adds up to is that barely a majority of eligible voters vote. This discrepancy overinflates the power of those who vote and lets a minority of people live under the illusion that it is the majority.

But in the end, the importance of voting far outweighs its problems. Voting is an example of how to participate in society or how to make a difference or an impact. Voting is tangible, voting is immediate, voting is relatively easy, and voting is the great equalizer. When people ask, "What can I do to change the world?" "Vote!" is an easy answer and the starting place for much greater social upheaval.

AMY RICHARDS is the author of *Opting In: Having a Child Without Losing Yourself* (Farrar, Straus and Giroux, 2008) and the coauthor of *Manifesta: Young Women, Feminism, and the Future* (Farrar, Straus and Giroux, 2000). Amy is also a cofounder of the Third Wave Foundation. (Photo credit: Ali Price)

★ ROB RIGGLE ★

DON'T LET THEM DECIDE FOR YOU . . .

Okay, take a moment and imagine the biggest losers you know. Really close your eyes and visualize them. Do you have a picture of them in your mind? Can you hear their voices, their conversations? What ridiculous things are they talking about, what asinine things are they saying to one another? Now, imagine these same people are making decisions for YOU. They, not you, are deciding the major issues that will affect your life and the lives of those you love—yet you might be willing to sit on the sidelines

and let these same people decide your future?!
Really?! Does that sound right to you?!!!

Basically, right now, one-third of Americans are
deciding how the other two-thirds will live. That's
the price you pay for not voting! And when you
consider what's at stake, these are the people
responsible for deciding whether or not we should
go to war; for levying and collecting taxes; for determining where our tax money will be spent . . . on
highways, health care, education, national security;
they're responsible for the seating of Supreme
Court justices and other federal judges. Put it all
together and it becomes crystal clear that Congress
and the executive branch have the power to control
large chunks of our lives!

And the price you pay for not being involved in
politics is to be governed by lesser men and/or
women than yourself.

Did I just blow your minds? Well, pull it

together because it's called democracy. We live in a wonderful nation that provides amazing freedom, but it requires active participation. It's really not that much to ask, when you think about it: caring about what happens to yourself and your neighbors and then acting on your conscience by following the issues and VOTING. That's not hard! Bankruptcy, unemployment, going to war . . . that's hard!

If you refuse to become involved in your surroundings, if you refuse to take part in your community, state, nation . . . world, then you really don't have a right to complain, do you? Democracies, and more specifically citizenship here in the United States, require participation, and the minimum requirement, in my opinion, is VOTING!

One look at history and it's clear that throughout the existence of man, men and women have struggled for the right to have a say in their own lives. This is a right that countless people have died trying to attain, and yet today it's a right that we enjoy simply because we are citizens of the United States of America. It's an amazing gift to actually have a vote, to have a say in what will happen in your life. For millions throughout the world today, this isn't the case. Close your eyes and imagine that existence for a moment. . . .

Don't waste this gift! Don't let others decide for you! Take the time to care about yourself and your neighbor. Vote . . . you'll always win if you do.

ROB RIGGLE is a correspondent on *The Daily Show with Jon Stewart.* He was a cast member on *Saturday Night Live* and appeared on *The Office* and *Arrested Development* and in films such as *Talladega Nights.* Prior to his life in comedy, Rob served in the United States Marine Corps and was deployed to Liberia, Albania, Kosovo, and Afghanistan. Rob was awarded more than nineteen medals and ribbons and promoted to the rank of major. He is still in the reserves today. (Photo courtesy of Comedy Central © 2007)

★ MARK RITCHIE ★

When I graduated from high school in 1968,
I was not old enough to vote. The voting age was
twenty-one; I was only sixteen. It was a tumul-
tuous time in our country's history. In Southeast
Asia, we were bogged down in a war with no clear
victory in sight. At home, we witnessed struggles
for civil rights, leaders being killed in the prime of
life, and the evils of segregation and Jim Crow. At
the same time, Rachel Carson's seminal work,
Silent Spring, raised awareness of the dangers of

chemical and pesticide use, sparking a global envi-ronmental movement. Presidential candidate Robert Kennedy traveled the country, reawakening the collective conscience of our nation and bringing the issue of extreme poverty out of the shadows. Tragically, he was murdered the summer following my graduation.

Millions of young people in 1968 threw them-selves into one or more of the social movements that characterized the decade. Petitions circulated on street corners everywhere, urging citizens to act on everything from ending discrimination against working women to ending the military draft. Young people marched in the streets across America protesting civil rights violations while others demanded justice for farm workers who planted and harvested much of our nation's food.

One of the most dramatic scenes of social change was playing out in the American South in the 1960s.

The voting rights movement was stirring and gathering into a giant force. Although I was raised in a small town in Iowa, I had a special interest in the civil rights struggle. I was born in the Deep South and spent many of my early summers living with my grandparents in Georgia. My grandparents farmed a tiny piece of land and supplemented their income by producing and repairing mattresses in a barn behind their farmhouse. Even as a child, one could not escape the reality of racial conflicts that embedded everyday life in the South. I rode with my grandfather as he picked up and delivered mattresses to many living in shantytowns. Images of the extreme poverty, especially on the faces of children, are forever seared in my memory.

As a young man, I grew increasingly active in civic engagement and politics. I joined in a national movement demanding the right to vote for eighteen year olds. There were many nineteen- and twenty-year-old soldiers sacrificing their lives in Vietnam, and none of them could vote. We believed that if we were old enough to be drafted and sent off to war, we were old enough to vote and have an equal voice in determining our future. In July 1971, eighteen year olds won the right to vote with the ratification of the 26th Amendment to the U.S. Constitution. It was a great victory, but we then needed to work harder to ensure that young adults actually exercised that right to vote.

In the early 1980s, I became active in a movement to save family farms and rural communities. The challenges facing Greater Minnesota had quickly ballooned into an economic disaster; reports of foreclosures and suicides in Minnesota became national news. During this important—yet challenging—time I had the opportunity to work closely with a political science professor from Carleton College named Paul Wellstone. A charismatic, natural leader, Paul Wellstone inspired a dedicated following of students and activists eager to help transform and improve our communities. Paul understood fully that in order to direct a new course in rural Minnesota, we needed to change state and federal laws that were devastating rural communities, including disastrous trade policies, predatory lending practices, and government-set low prices. Paul also recognized that if we were going to change these policies, we needed to change the policymakers.

Paul Wellstone was a strong believer in the need for voter registration and "Get Out the Vote" drives. He taught me that every voice—and vote—mattered and that everyone should be included in the political process. He encouraged civic activists to move beyond issue-specific organizing and to consider running for elected office. I remember late-night conversations where he strongly made this case to me.

In 1990, Paul Wellstone shocked the political establishment by winning a seat in the U.S. Senate, defeating an entrenched incumbent that outspent him 10 to 1. Paul's success was a source of pure joy for so many people. But his accomplishment was also a lesson. He was able to run a political campaign true to his values and win. If someone that honest, caring, and committed could get elected, others were encouraged to do the same. I was proud of Paul, happy to have been part of the movement that elected him, and eager to work with him on moving Minnesota and our country ahead.

On October 25, 2002, while in Kentucky preparing for a speech related to the importance of family farms and rural communities, I learned of the tragic plane crash that took the lives of Paul; his wife, Sheila; his daughter; as well as staff. I had lost a dear friend.

Paul's death was a true turning point in my life.

I began asking myself seriously where I was headed in my life and what else I needed to be doing to make a difference in this world. Recalling those late-night talks with Paul, I decided to take a leave of absence from my work as president of the Institute for Agriculture and Trade Policy, a non-profit think tank that I had led for twenty years, to work on a massive voter registration campaign called NOVEMBER 2. It was a huge success. More than two thousand groups helped register five million people, making it was one of the largest nonpartisan voter mobilizations in our nation's history. I even got a chance to be on *The Daily Show* on election night in 2004.

But this was only the beginning of the process for me. While I was happy with the success of our work on the NOVEMBER 2 campaign, I became increasingly concerned about the integrity of elections. Inspired by my friend and mentor, I filed to run for secretary of state in Minnesota, a position responsible for overseeing elections in the state. On November 7, 2006, I was elected.

As I have grown older, I have come to understand how our actions can effect real change. I believe strongly that it is so important that we vote in every election. It is not only our right but also our chance to have our voices heard in how we want to be governed and what we want our future to be. Electoral politics is not perfection; it is about bending the arc of history toward justice, as Rev. Dr. Martin Luther King Jr. called on us to do. Sitting idly by, criticizing the news of the day, will get us nowhere. Voting is a powerful affirmation of the fundamental promise of liberty and justice for all.

MARK RITCHIE is Minnesota's secretary of state. He works with local election officials and civic groups to make sure that Minnesota remains the top state in the nation for voter turnout and a national leader in the conduct of fair, open, and secure elections. In 2004, Mark led National Voice and NOVEMBER 2 to register over five million new voters, one of the largest voter mobilizations in American history.

★ HENRY ROLLINS ★

If you look at American history, you will find that for many Americans, the right to vote took a long time to arrive and was met by some with great resistance. It's hard to imagine that, in America, the right to vote would even be up for discussion, but up until the late part of the nineteenth century, women and African Americans were kept away from the ballot box. For other minorities voting rights took even longer. From this one could surmise that Democracy as we know it now was not on the minds of everyone in America and for some, was a compromise. Caving in to the notion of equality was enough to start a war.

In the early days of the civil rights movement, when people like Medgar Evers went door-to-door in the South, reminding African Americans that they had the right to vote and should do so, quite often the Ku Klux Klan was quick to pay a follow-up visit to the same residences to inform them that if they did vote, things could go very badly for them.

The above examples show just how potent a citizen's vote is. If it wasn't, there wouldn't have been so much energy expended over the centuries to make sure that many did not vote or that their votes were not counted. If anything, this battle should be an indicator as to just how fragile Democracy is and how vigilantly it should be protected, maintained, and never taken for granted. Democracy has been called by some a social experiment, and I guess that any system of governance is. As far as I can tell, it's the fairest and most decent way to run the show—or at least the rule book that I feel the most comfortable with. If America were to lose Democracy, I would be afraid of what would take its place—very afraid.

You would think that on voting day, offices would be empty and stores would be on holiday hours to accommodate the millions of Americans lining up to cast their ballots. You would think that in the spirit of fair play and for the good of the nation, people wouldn't have to wait for hours in long, seemingly endless lines, like Stalin-era Soviets hoping for bread, just to cast their votes. You would hope this to be true but it's not and that has to change, and I think it will.

As fragile as Democracy is, I believe it will survive the few who subvert it to deprive the many of its brilliant potential.

Besides wanting to have my say in this great country, the main reason I vote is because I believe there are some who would prefer I did not. Hell, that makes it downright fun. By voting, we clear the air and further define and strengthen Democracy. The constant problem Democracy faces is politicians. What a bunch these folks are! By voting and letting them know what's on our minds, we remind them who they work for and whose interests they serve, lest they forget for one second. Successful politicians strive to appear trustworthy and confident, attracting votes to their column. I wish they would also exhibit a healthy amount of fear of failure at their post and of the people they represent.

Voting is one of the greatest opportunities we have to keep us safe and moving forward. Why that wouldn't be of the greatest importance to everyone is beyond me. Do it.

HENRY ROLLINS was the vocalist for the band Black Flag, and now tours the world with his own Rollins Band, as a public speaker, and on behalf of the USO. The Grammy-winning performer, author, and actor also hosts IFC's *The Henry Rollins Show*, introduces listeners to hidden gems on his weekly radio show, and runs his publishing company, 2-13-61. (Photo credit: Maura Lanahan)

★ ROMEO ★

WHY I WANT TO VOTE

I turned eighteen over the summer, and I can't wait to vote. My friends and I made a pact that when we turned eighteen, we would all register to vote together. 2008 could be a historic election, so it's a good time to be in the mix. Voting is important because I know how much each vote counts. My parents instilled in me the belief that my opinion matters and it matters partly because, as young people, we have influence. Being able to vote makes you feel grown-up. It is a part of the growing process to recognize that we have the power to shape the future. We have the most at stake, and we are the leaders of the future. We need to get out and vote to choose the person that we think is going to get everything straight. We are account-able for choosing the person that will lead us and look out for us; for electing someone into office who views life optimistically, the way I do—the way most of us do. Some of our biggest concerns are war, race issues, and the economy. Politics has even begun playing a role in the state of hip-hop. . . . We have to be heard and become a part of the solution, not perpetuate the problem.

Being a teenager can be fun, but it also involves knowing your responsibilities. We all want to grow up so that we can do what we want, but we need to make sure that we are about something. There are so many things thrown at us and so many decisions to make; if you are not a strong person, you can be led down the wrong path. Peer pressure is always discussed in a negative sense, but I think peer pressure can be a positive, too. I want to pressure my peers. . . . Get off the couch! Go vote! Go make a difference!

When I walk into the voting booth on Election Day, I know I'll feel like Superman when I walk out.

ROMEO MILLER (aka Lil' Romeo) is an actor, rapper, basketball star, and entrepreneur. He has released six albums and is the author of *Guaranteed Success for Teens* (Urban Books, 2008). He will play basketball for the University of Southern California starting in the fall of 2008. The oldest of seven children, Romeo is originally from New Orleans. (Photo credit: Tom Blankenship)

★ ATOOSA RUBENSTEIN ★

For the longest time, I couldn't have cared
less about the political process. It was sort of like
happening over *there* while my life was happening
over *here*. Does that sound familiar at all? I was so
self-absorbed. My main goals in life were being
successful, getting recognized for it, and looking
as good as possible when that recognition would
come . . . superficial, superficial, and more superficial.
I know—puke.com.

The one thing that wasn't frivolous, though, was

the connection I felt to my girls—the millions and millions of teenage girls who had come into my life as a result of my job as editor-in-chief of *CosmoGIRL!* and then, *Seventeen.* I call them Alpha Kitties, because they're powerful and unafraid—but still glamorous, like cats! This tribe of AKs had given me an incredible life that I'd never thought I'd have, and so I was forever indebted to them. If you ask anyone who ever worked with me, they'll attest that my commitment and sense of responsibility to my girls was so powerful it couldn't be faked. This relationship was far from superficial— as a contrast to the rest of my life. But sure, the *basis* of our relationship was firmly rooted in fluff. Come on—we talked about clothes, makeup, and hairstyles. Sure, there was some serious and deep stuff thrown in there, but for the most part it was a fun pajama party.

But then the world began to change—9/11, the

tsunami, Hurricane Katrina—and with it, a new status quo for Americans: an overall dreadful feeling of Okay-God-What's-Next?

I don't know if you relate, but I was so scared, I ignored what was happening in the world. Celebrity gossip got juicy just at the right time: it was so much easier to watch than the regular news. After all, how could *I* make a difference? Well, that's how I felt, until . . . I saw the movie *An Inconvenient Truth.* I went to the screening with one of my *most* fashion-y friends—after all, Al Gore was sort of chic. We wanted to see what it was all about. Now, if you haven't seen the movie yet, you must. Trust me when I tell you, it was the scariest movie I've ever seen: scarier than *Saw.* Scarier than anything. Except . . . it was *real.* And yet the first comment my friend made was, "We'd better do a photo shoot in Greenland before it totally melts!" That was a major epiphany. What the hell was

I doing burying my head in designer clothes? I realized at that very moment that being the cool big sister with the best style advice was no longer enough. My girls needed a *new* kind of big sister—and I needed to become more knowledgeable, more aware . . . and fast. I wasn't smart enough, and the world is a scary place.

I left my job as editor-in-chief and started a journey. I needed to figure out what us Alpha Kitties could do to bring peace, love, and change to the world. During this process (I'm still in it!), I've learned how important our local and national leadership is.

One of the things that freaked me out in the movie (and even more so, once I started really reading up on it) is how money oriented government—and in turn, the election process—has gotten. Every time I see a commercial for a new drug on the market, I'm incredibly suspect. It almost seems as though diseases are being created so that some drug companies can make more money by getting us hooked on their products—and the government is allowing this to happen because those same companies are some of the biggest campaign donors. That's just one example, but my point is, we need to take big business out of government so that we can really protect the people and this land that our ancestors (well, not mine! I'm an immigrant!) fought so hard to secure for us.

Yes, as citizens we *can* make a difference—especially with regard to the environment and climate change—by adopting better habits. But we're working against a powerful force if our government doesn't make smart policy choices that further protect us. And if we're so absorbed in our own lives and celebrity gossip, the big businesses will keep voting in government officials that suit *their* purposes. And us? Well, we'll always have Paris . . . Hilton. That is, until the state of the world becomes so serious, dangerous, and life-threatening that we actually won't *care* about her or the other celebutards anymore. And then? The only people we can blame for not being involved in the process and getting people elected who really *do* speak for us are ourselves. The companies with the big money? You can bet they are making sure their interests are heard in Washington. But what about you and me? We may not have the zillions of dollars, but the one thing we do have? A vote. Let's make it count.

ATOOSA RUBENSTEIN started Big Momma Productions, Inc., in December 2006. She was formerly editor-in-chief of *Seventeen*, and the creator and executive producer of MTV's *Miss Seventeen*. At age twenty-six she founded and served as the editor-in-chief of *CosmoGIRL!*, making her the youngest editor in the history of Hearst Magazine. She got her start as an intern at *Sassy* magazine. Visit her online at www.atoosa.com.

★ STUART SCOTT ★

YOU MATTER

How many times do you stand around . . . make

a joke about your politicians . . . call them clowns—

　—how often do you complain . . . "Yo, this ain't

right—dude's playin' games"

　—it's the DIS-DAIN . . . in . . . your . . . voice . . .

that almost claims . . . "YOU DON'T MATTER"

　—how you gonna scream and shout . . . and talk

ABOUT the man leading this country . . . YOUR

country . . . and sit there and do NOTHING?

　—please . . . "nothing" amounts to SOME-

THING . . . SOMETHING amounts to INDIF-
FERENCE . . . INDIFFERENCE amounts to
LAZINESS

—and it IS this attitude that keeps you twisted
and wrong . . . singin' a song about "how the man
is keeping you down?"—think about it . . . who's
the clown??—i know . . . you're young, strong . . .
tryin' to get down . . . do your thing . . . hittin' the
town . . . trying to make it in this huge world . . .
but remember . . . it is YOUR HUGE WORLD—
and if you don't like how "the man" flows—stop
talking about your own WOES . . . and change it
. . . how often do you vote???—it ain't no joke—how
many times . . . have you CARED enough to walk
in a booth . . . speak your own TRUTH . . . what??
. . . it's not cool?? . . . a little UNCOUTH??—you
wanna change the world . . . make your own life
SWIRL in new and different ways?? . . . then stop
thinkin' about just gettin' PAID

—expand your thoughts . . . think outside a box—and the act of voting only LOCKS . . . you up for an hour on a day . . . ONE DAY . . . to HAVE A SAY . . . if the millions of young people can change the course of a new-release movie . . . hit the cinemas in droves . . . drive the box office SILLY . . . then can't WE—also affect who leads us???

IMAGINE—every young twenty-somethin' . . . takes three hours for a flick . . . makes the film the number one HIT . . . imagine if they also went to VOTE . . . less time . . . less energy . . . MORE IMPACT . . . the demographic that drives our economy . . . the 18-to-34 . . . can do MORE than just SPEND . . . they can WIN . . . the right to decide who the man . . . or the WOMAN will be . . . it's right there . . . but you gotta SEE . . . it clearly . . . we only have THIS world . . . our world . . . and I'm told . . . YOU . . . actually DO matter . . . PROVE IT . . . spoken word.

STUART SCOTT is a sportscaster for ESPN. He anchors *SportsCenter* and hosts *NFL PrimeTime*, and is also a courtside reporter for the NBA. He has interviewed major figures such as Michael Jordan, Tiger Woods, Sammy Sosa, and Bill Clinton. Scott attended the University of North Carolina, where he majored in speech communications and radio, television, and motion pictures. (Photo © Chris Farina/Corbis)

★ HOLLY SHULMAN ★

You do things that make a difference in the world every day. You recycle. You raise money for charity. You carpool to save fuel. You sign a petition, and you boycott a company whose principles you don't agree with. But now you've turned eighteen and you have a chance to make an even greater difference. You get to vote.

On a small scale, you've been making a difference, but imagine the difference your day-to-day actions would have if you had the force of a whole government behind you with 435 representatives, 100 senators, and a president working for *you* on the issues that matter to *you* the most. The boycott you participated in helped show a company that uses sweatshop labor that you won't stand for it, and it made a little difference. But if you vote for a leader who will write a law that will ban the sale of sweatshop-made goods in the U.S., you've made a big difference that will echo around the world.

The biggest issues often affect young people the most. Now, in Iraq young soldiers are dying, tuition and student loans rates are skyrocketing, and what used to be American jobs are moving halfway around the world. You will one day inherit an earth that's been through a lot: from climate change to deforestation to fuel overconsumption and more. With so many big problems, you need big solutions.

Part of growing up is figuring out which are the

problems you can solve all on your own and which are the ones for which you need to ask help from others. These aren't the kinds of problems that you can solve all on your own. Some of these aren't even the types of problems that the United States can solve all on its own, but they are all problems that we can get closer to solving with leadership that cares about these issues—leaders that you have an opportunity to elect.

So if you want to solve your problems, continue doing what you're doing: keep watching the news, donating to charity, saving fuel, recycling, and more. But now you have a special opportunity—a right—to have some help solving your big problems. You have the right and the privilege to elect someone to help you out, to represent your interests in Congress, in the Senate, in the Presidency, someone with all of the resources of government behind him or her. Someone who has the resources to make big changes, even for young people. But they'll only do it if you ask.

HOLLY SHULMAN, twenty-five, has worked on political campaigns, and advocacy campaigns and is the founder of Vote Against Violence, an organization dedicated to electing candidates who will work to end domestic and sexual violence. She has also served as Political Director of the Women's Information Network, a networking organization for young pro-choice Democratic women. Originally from Demarest, New Jersey, Holly is a graduate of Vassar College. (Photo credit: Jonathan Zuck)

★ PETER SÍS ★

PETER SÍS is an acclaimed author, illustrator, and filmmaker. He was born in Czechoslovakia and grew up under communist rule. He spent his childhood drawing and also embraced music, becoming a deejay and serving as an emcee for the Beach Boys on their European tour. Peter moved to the United States in 1982, and his work frequently explores themes of artistic freedom. He was named a MacArthur Fellow in 2003 and has contributed editorial illustrations to *The Atlantic Monthly, Time, Newsweek, Esquire,* and *The New York Times Book Review,* which has published one thousand of his drawings. (Photo credit: David Port)

★ AMBER TAMBLYN ★

In 2000 I was seventeen years old. I missed the presidential election by a few months and took it like a dodgeball to the stomach. To me, voting was the ultimate choice. It wasn't so much my history teacher in high school or my relatives who made me interested in the Art of Voting. (Yeah, I said ART. Deal with it.) It was the sense that I was becoming a part of something that was bigger than I am—a rare opportunity for someone who has been acting since the age of nine and has learned how to live vicariously through herself. I was ready to go beyond all that. I wanted so badly to be a new tooth in the mouth of my country, helping to grind into the term *democracy*, by really becoming a part of the nutritional value of it: US. The people. The nine-to-fivers who take thirty-minute intermissions on an Election Day to be sincere. To mean what we say.

I volunteered at my local polling place that election, helping to sign off names and give out the ballots. For me, it was never about politics. It was always about the Choice, something my parents raised me to believe I did, and would always, have. I never took that for granted.

Pancakes instead of waffles for breakfast kind of Choice. Moth taming instead of butterfly killing kind of Choice. She-Ra instead of Barbie kind of Choice. Telling Elizabeth Nolan I broke her glass animal instead of blaming an imaginary earthquake kind of Choice. Monkey bars so I could have strong arms instead of swings kind of Choice. Pillow punching instead of punching the boy who wouldn't kiss me in third grade kind of Choice. Writing my senator about why he should help save the gray wolf in California instead of playing with my wolf stuffed animals Choice. Saying good-bye to my uncle with my heart instead of my eyes at his open-casket funeral Choice. Submitting poems instead of college applications Choice. Travis Browner instead of the one who got good grades Choice. Picking up a picket sign instead of that hitchhiker guy on the I-5 Choice. Getting in the car with a friend after she'd been drinking instead of just getting in the passenger seat Choice. Talking to the gothic girl at the airport with the sad teleportation eyes screaming, "Take me away from here!" Choice. Cutting communication with the long-distance lover who left me with a paper trail of tears Choice.

Driving straight because both left and right looked sketchy Choice. Picking up trash for Heal the Bay the day before the Emmys instead of more silly self-pampering Choice. Registering to vote the day I turned 18, instead of spending my time telling people why they should vote Choice. Sitting here and sharing my history with you, the reader, in the hopes that, when it comes to your own history, you will find there is no other choice but Choice.

Mindy Nettifee once wrote, "You don't survive history, history survives you." It's true. It's not what you believe or think. It's what you do. What you choose.

Plus, you get that super rad I VOTED sticker with the stars and colors that will make your underage siblings blind with jealousy, the way I once was when I was seventeen. Say to them, "Oh this ol' thing? It's just my BONA FIDE HISTORIC CONTRIBUTION TO YOUR FUTURE. Don't worry, kid. You'll get your time." Yes, we will. Don't ever let it pass you by.

AMBER TAMBLYN is an actor best known for her roles in *Joan of Arcadia* and *The Sisterhood of the Traveling Pants*. She is the author of *Free Stallions*, a book of poetry, and her writing also appears in a number of magazines, including *Nylon*. She lives in Los Angeles. Visit her online at www.amtam.com and www.rebelasylum.com.

★ AARON TANG ★

WHY VOTING SHOULD MATTER TO YOUNG PEOPLE THIS NOVEMBER

There are two ways one might account for America's persistent and reckless neglect of millions of our children. One way is to attribute our failures—one million students who drop out of school each year; nine million children without health insurance; eleven million who attend schools with facilities in inadequate condition; and thirteen million who live beneath the poverty line—to a lack of technical know-how. Perhaps we *want* to provide children with the educational, health, and developmental supports they need to succeed, but we lack the policy and operational expertise to do so.

A second explanation for our failures would be to attribute them to a shortage of political will. Maybe we actually *do* know what good schools, health services, and support systems would look like for *all* children, but we've failed to provide them because the public and our elected officials deem other things to be of greater importance. If this is the case, what is needed in Washington, DC, is a major infusion of voices and votes to demand that what is best for children finally be put first.

After five years working across the country with thousands of high-school and college-age members of Our Education, a national youth advocacy organization I cofounded with peers at Yale University in 2003, I am convinced that our nation's disregard for millions of our youth owes to the second explanation, not the first. There are too many examples of successful programs serving low-income children—like the State Children's Health Insurance Program (SCHIP) first enacted in 1997, and like the high-performing KIPP (Knowledge Is Power Program) public charter schools in fifty-seven under-resourced communities—for us to blame a lack of technical expertise. And there are too few examples of officials who make good on their promises to put children at the top of their legislative priorities for us to let politicians off the hook.

The failure of Congress in October 2007 to extend SCHIP insurance to as many as four million of our nine million uninsured children is a perfect example of America's deficit of political will to do right by children. In a nation that ranks second worst in the developed world for infant mortality rates (the American average is two and a half times that of Finland, Iceland, or Norway), improving health coverage for children is a glaring problem with an equally obvious solution. Moreover, the expansion of SCHIP would have had a neutral effect on the ballooning federal deficit, since it would have been paid for by a tax on cigarettes of 61 cents per pack. Yet the proposal, which passed by a 114-vote majority in the House and a 34-vote majority in the Senate, was vetoed by the president and did not have the required two-thirds majority support in Congress for an override.

Why wasn't there enough political resolve to take care of millions of sick and injured children? By the same token, why does federal education spending continue to trail military spending by 15 to 1? The simplest, short answer is that the greatest strength of our democratic system is also its greatest weakness: in American politics, the squeakiest wheel gets the grease. The voting blocs, interest groups, and lobbyists who complain the loudest are also the ones who are most likely to have their demands and concerns addressed.

Who is left out in this call-and-response dynamic of representative politics? Those who have little—or worse yet, no—voice. America's history is replete with examples of groups of disenfranchised people who, by virtue of their lack of political say-so, do not have the opportunity to earn their share of our country's incredible prosperity. African Americans (both during and after slavery), non-land-owning whites, women, Native Americans, and various immigrant populations have all seen their rights trampled upon and best interests ignored over the past two and a half centuries. And though we may be a long time removed from the days when outright slavery, misogyny, and racism were a normal part of everyday American life, there are still significant swaths of the population who do not yet have sufficient say in our democracy—and who suffer the consequences direly.

Chief among these groups of disenfranchised peoples are children and adolescents. Because children do not vote, much less contribute to political campaigns and interest groups, they are beholden to the policies put in place by officials and driven by the broader public opinion, both of which they rarely can influence. And unfortunately for these youth, America does not have a "put the children first" attitude.

But we can change that. As a generation of young voters who remember vividly what it is like to be a child and who are sensitized to the variety of issues and pressures facing kids both inside and outside of school, we have the power to pressure our officials to do right by youth. College affordability, K–12 education reform, children's health insurance, the future of *our* social security: all of these issues are paramount to ensuring our nation's long-term health. Yet precious few politicians and adult voters are acting on them with the urgency that is needed.

We, as young voters, can step up and bring attention to these issues that have been out of the public limelight. And here is a vision for the kind of society that we can work toward, and that our votes can bring about. Among the Masai people, a famous tribe in eastern Africa, the traditional greeting passed between both friends and strangers is "Kasserian ingera?" which means, "How are the children?" It is a reflection of the Masai people's priorities. Family members who have not seen one another in years ask first about the well-being of one anothers' children. Visitors from far-off villages, when arriving in a new place, inquire as to the welfare of the children before anything else. To the Masai, life is good when the children are well, because nothing is more important than their health, their education, their safety.

I wonder what would America look like if our politicians asked one another, "How are the children?" before debating an Iraq war resolution, a renewable energy bill, an environmental preservation act? Would the best interests of children finally trump special interests and ideology in a future version of the No Child Left Behind Act or on a future vote over SCHIP? There's only one way to find out, one way to send a message loud and clear to our leaders: let's show up in numbers at the ballot box this November and vote for the city council members, state legislators, congresspeople, senators, and yes, the presidential candidate who promises, before any other question, to answer ours: "How are the children?"

AARON TANG is the cofounder and codirector of Our Education (www.OurEd.org), a national nonprofit working to build a national youth movement for quality public education. He is a graduate of public schools in Painesville, Ohio; a 2004 Truman Scholar; 2005 *USA Today* All-USA College Academic First Team honoree; 2005 Echoing Green Fellow, and recipient of the Yale University's 2005 Alpheus Henry Snow Prize. (Photo credit: Liz Campbell)

★ AISHA TYLER ★

I am very grateful for the opportunities I get to speak out on a national platform on behalf of issues and causes I care about: the environment, battered women and children, social injustice and inequality. It is one of the best perks of my job and, in my opinion, the best side effect of celebrity: the opportunity to help others simply by showing up, by speaking out. People sometimes criticize celebrities for making political statements, for using their name recognition as a pulpit. They say, "Who the hell are they to tell us what they think? What makes them so special?" And you know what? They're right. Celebrities *aren't* special. We're just Americans —like you, like everyone else. We care about the direction of our country, about its promise and its failings, just like everyone else. And when it comes to speaking out, to getting involved in politics, and to voting, we're all celebrities— because each of our votes counts equally, and each is equally valuable.

The thing is that voting, getting involved, speaking out for causes you believe in, aren't special privileges reserved for politicians and celebrities. All of us have not just the right, but the *responsibility* to stand up, to speak out—when we see injustice, or suffering, or inequality. You don't have to be famous to make a difference. All you have to do is care. Your opinion matters just as much as mine, or Bono's, or a senator's, or anyone else's. The beauty, and the burden, of the American system is our extraordinary right to be heard. Lift that burden up, and live up to the extraordinary promise you have inside. Your voice is important, it is meaningful, and it is powerful. To unlock that power, all you have to do is use it. Be your own celebrity. Vote.

AISHA TYLER is an actor, comedian, and philanthropist. She has appeared in many television shows and movies, and is currently preparing to direct her first film, from an original screenplay she wrote. Aisha Tyler recently published her first nonfiction book, entitled *Swerve: Reckless Observations of a Postmodern Girl*, and has had several articles published in national magazines such as *Glamour, Oprah, Jane,* and *Movieline.* (Photo credit: Kevin Scott Hees)

★ GABRIELLE UNION ★

WHAT REALLY MADE ME REALIZE THE
IMPORTANCE OF VOTING . . .

. . . was when I realized the amount of power it gives you. Not power in the sense that you are preparing to take over the world, but the amount of power that gave me a voice and that meant that someone was listening to it. It was my first real feeling of being *empowered.*

Aside from what I knew about my history and racism, I can remember growing up hearing stories about how people were harassed and taunted on their way to the polls to try and keep them from voting. People with so much hatred that they would attempt to devalue the rights of another human being and keep them from being heard. I had not experienced that. So, as much as I knew it to be true, it was a hard pill to swallow. I was voting for Most Popular, Most Likely to Succeed, and Best Legs (I won that one), and no one was trying to keep me from casting my vote. Those were the fun moments, but deep down I knew there were more important things than that.

When I turned eighteen and could register to vote, what my rights meant became invaluable to me. Not only was I now of the legal age to register and to vote, but I was being *encouraged* to do so. I was no longer considered a child. I was now an adult with an opinion regarding who would be the leader of my country and some power as to how it would be led. I was being asked to step up and be heard! I was told that what I had to say was of importance to someone other than myself. My voice was now worthy of a respect that I had not known before. Admittedly, I was excited. I enjoyed the impact that I would make by showing up, being counted, and making my voice heard. I was prepared to wear my I VOTED sticker with pride.

When we are young we always want to be independent, to be an adult, to be anything other than a child. We want to go on dates, determine our curfew, have a car, and have our own money. Adulthood meant independence, being able to do the fun things, not always asking for permission. Adulthood to me also meant being responsible and accountable for myself and my actions. I looked at voting as a responsibility, and it was something that I wanted to do. I wanted to understand what was important to me, what I stood for, and what I valued.

Being able to vote is something that I have

always treasured. It was something that I looked forward to with the same passion and excitement as graduating college, beginning my career, and buying a home. It was one of the biggest statements of my adult life, of my responsibility, of my independence. It is a statement that gives me strength and shows me who I am as a person, as a woman, and as a citizen.

The power that I get from voting is a reminder of our history and the historical figures that fought for my voice, my opinion, and my independence. Voting is a constant reminder of where we were, how far we have come, and where we are going. This is power that I do not take for granted, but that I am reminded to embrace. This statement of my power is one that I value and hope never to lose and one that I will continue to share with others. It is *my voice* that I will share . . . with anyone who is willing to listen.

GABRIELLE UNION is a film and television actor and former model. She has been nominated for many awards, and won Best Supporting Actress for her role in *Bring It On* at the 2001 Black Reel Awards. She is also an activist who is involved in combating violence against women. Gabrielle graduated with honors from UCLA with a degree in sociology.

★ SARA VARON ★
&
★ SHEILA O'DONNELL ★

SARA VARON (right) is an illustrator/printmaker/comics artist currently living in Brooklyn, New York. Her books include *Chicken and Cat* (Scholastic Press, 2006) and *Robot Dreams* (First Second Books, 2007). Sheila O'Donnell (left), the author of the comic in this book, is her oldest and favorite friend.

SHEILA O'DONNELL is a writer with a day job raising money for social and economic justice in Chicago, Illinois. She is happy to collaborate with her oldest and best friend, Sara, on this important project.

Voting makes me part of something bigger. I am only one small person, but when I vote I think about everyone else, across the country, making decisions that will impact us all.

★ ALICE WALKER ★

MY FATHER'S VOTE

Interestingly I don't remember the first time I voted but I remember the first time my father did. It was in 1932, twelve years before I was born. He wanted desperately to ensure a better life for his wife and "houseful of children" and so he hoped to vote for Franklin Delano Roosevelt, whom he believed would alleviate the worst hardships of the Great Depression from which much of the country was suffering. My father never considered leaving his family, or leaving the South, as many did during those years. He loved us very much; he also loved the land, where Walkers had lived for generations. He hunted and fished in the woods, worked the plantations and fields, and was never happy to be more than a few miles from the area his father—his best and closest buddy—still lived, and where he had been born.

And so, though three white men with shotguns sat on the porch of the country store, which was the voting place, and though it was well known they'd vowed to shoot down any black man who dared to attempt to vote, my father, thinking of his family, and especially of his hungry children, walked past them, and voted. The first black man in the county, unconnected to white power or lineage, to do so.

It was this memory that sent me, years later, to Liberty County, Georgia, to help register voters when I was in college, and later to Mississippi to do the same as an adult.

In Mississippi I encountered many people who resembled my dad: men and women, resisting the violence and poverty of their lives under American apartheid, who walked directly into the line of danger in an attempt to improve the lives of themselves and those of their families. When I arrived there the stories that met me were horrendous: a would-be voter whose blown-out brains lay where they fell underneath the wheels of a white man's truck. The firebombing of the home of Vernon Dahmer, a voting rights activist whose wife, along with Dahmer, was killed. The recently recovered bodies of three young men—James Cheney, Michael Schwerner, and Andrew Goodman—who had been tortured and murdered by the Ku Klux Klan (who doubled as local officials), and buried under an earthen dam in the countryside.

I was amazed to see that, like my father, the black people in Mississippi never considered turning back. Holding their loved ones and their children very dear, they persevered. They wanted a say in the running of their lives. They wanted the vote. Thrown out of their houses, banished from land they'd worked all their lives, beaten and some-times broken, they steadily rose and marched or staggered to the ballot box. I fell quite in love with them. To this day I consider them a human sunrise; their rising, like the sun itself, warming, irresistible, and profound.

Carrying my father's courage and deep compas-sion for his family and neighbors—all suffering so cruelly during the Depression—ever in my heart, I vote. Terrible and disappointing people have been elected and selected to govern in America and I am far from unburdened by this fact. However, when-ever I vote I know I am voting for the idea of democracy, that some day all of us may have it. I am voting for the beauty and resilience, the deep bravery of the people of Mississippi. And yes, I am voting for my dad.

ALICE WALKER is known for her literary fiction, including the Pulitzer Prize–winning *The Color Purple* (now a major Broadway play), her many volumes of poetry, and her powerful nonfiction collections. In the fall of 2006 she published a book of spiritual ruminations with a progressive political edge: *We Are the Ones We Have Been Waiting For: Inner Light in a Time of Darkness.* Ms. Walker has also published several children's books, including *There Is a Flower at the Tip of My Nose Smelling Me* and *Why War Is Never a Good Idea.* Ms. Walker was inducted into the California Hall of Fame in December 2006. (Photo credit: Andrea Roth)

★ JOAN WALSH ★

I'm not sure if the story of the first time I voted is a tale of courage or betrayal. I'll have to let the reader decide. But I think it will tell you how much voting means to me.

I turned eighteen in 1976, the year Jimmy Carter challenged Jerry Ford for the presidency. Everything I know about politics I learned from my father, who was a staunch supporter of civil rights and a lifelong Democrat. But he just didn't like Jimmy Carter—he wasn't liberal enough, and my father, though a Catholic, was suspicious of people who wore their religion on their political sleeve. He also respected Ford for restoring the office of the presidency after the nightmare of Watergate. We argued about the coming election for weeks—I couldn't believe he would even think of voting Republican! —and finally we came up with a compromise: since our votes would cancel each other out if I went for Carter and he went for Ford, why didn't we both vote for Eugene McCarthy, the Democrat who ran a famous antiwar campaign in 1968, who was running an independent campaign for president that year?

Now, all these years later, I can't believe we even considered this. I still blame the Green Party, as well as voters who stayed home, for Al Gore's loss to George W. Bush in 2000. But at eighteen, I thought the idea daring. I like the notion of my father and I uniting to cast a protest vote, rather than settling for the lesser of two evils.

Or at least I liked it until I went into the voting booth. There in the public library of my Wisconsin suburb, I thought about how close the race was and how much was at a stake. Selfishly, or not, I really wanted my first vote to mean something. I got a little bit teary thinking about the years women couldn't vote, the years—not all that long ago, in 1976—when African Americans were kept away from the polls (I still have those thoughts and feelings every Election Day). I mulled my decision for what seemed like forever, and finally I decided I couldn't throw away my vote on a protest. I believed Jimmy Carter would be a better president than Jerry Ford. So I voted for Carter and went outside to face the music with my dad.

He wasn't angry at me. I think he appreciated that he'd taken me through an unforgettable learning experience, and he respected that in the end, I couldn't trade my vote away. He'd gone ahead and voted for McCarthy. I still regret not keeping my word to my father, but I'm happy I voted my conscience. And since Carter is one of only two successful presidential candidates I've ever voted for (three, if you count Al Gore!) I'm glad I did it.

In January 2008 my daughter turned eighteen. She was lucky enough to have had a woman and African American (Hillary Clinton and Barack Obama) on California's Democratic primary ballot in February. I'm not going to try any horse-trading with her, but I hope I can find as memorable a way to impress on her the importance of voting as my father found for me.

JOAN WALSH is editor in chief at Salon.com. Her work has appeared in many national publications, winning her a 2004 Western Magazine Award. She has also worked as a consultant to national and regional foundations. She is the author of *Splash Hit: The Pacific Bell Park Story* (Chronicle Books, 2001) and *Stories of Renewal: Community Building and the Future of Urban America* (Rockefeller Foundation, 1997). (Photo credit: Dwayne Newton)

★ Marcellus Wiley ★

In my teenage years, I was quick to point toward outer circumstances and blame others for any shortcomings that existed in my reality. Now that I'm thirty-three years old, I have learned, sometimes the hard way, to put a strong emphasis on *my* actions and intentions when it comes to my life's outcome.

I have learned from my lessons in life the importance of my signature. Yes, metaphorically, the simple task of writing my name is one of the most powerful displays of my uniqueness that was given to me. My signature is one of God's ways of distinguishing me from any other person on this planet—past, present, or future. Just as people touch one another and are identified with unique fingerprints, their signatures carry a unique power that must be expressed, must be recognized. This is the same power that's utilized when voting.

Voting is your way of expressing to all that you are grateful for the rights and opportunity to make a difference with your single voice. Yes, voting is necessary.

In today's world, our voices are being muted by so many sensational issues and platforms, that the masses are feeling irrelevant, feeling less than equal. As the rich get richer, the rift in our economic classes grows wider by the moment. The ultimate equalizer is voting. Voting is your opportunity to scream out your opinion on any vast number of issues. The voting booth is one of the few remaining places where there is a level playing field. In the voting booth, every man and woman are still considered equal.

Our modern technological advances have provided Americans with every opportunity imaginable to voice their opinion. You can form social groups in protest, telephone political radio and TV shows in disgust or support, even write a blog to evoke a collective opinion, in hopes of rallying those with like minds. But, despite all the advances we have in media and its platforms that embrace and beg for our attention, nothing comes close to enforcing change like the power of your single vote.

I know it can be discouraging at times, in the midst of the present conditions, to wonder if change is possible. A reality of life is that nothing stays the same; either it gets better or it gets worse. Voting is your way to help sway that force of movement toward the positive. By not voicing your opinion, you are yelling to the world, "I don't care!" That sentiment certainly won't lead our nation in the right direction. Take your hands off the steering wheel in this race and we are certain to crash!

The mere existence of present-day circumstances such as poverty, violence, the mortgage crisis, the senselessness and expense of the Iraq war, etc., all weighs heavy on our hearts. But honestly ask yourself as the 2008 elections near and you have the opportunity to flex your power: are you going to stay Bitter or are you going to be Better? How are you going to harness all of your thoughts, opinions, and beliefs into actual action? The difference maker is *you* standing in that election booth.

You should never feel, or let anyone or anything else make you feel as if you don't matter. The following analogy helps illustrate that point.

If you were to have a million dollars in your

possession—yes, one million one-dollar bills—you know what they would call you, right? Yes, a millionaire! However, if you were to lose one—just one—of those dollar bills, you know what they would call you then? I don't know, either, but it surely wouldn't be a millionaire! My point is to show you the power of one, the power of you! You are that single one-dollar bill that may seem of little value to you, but if expressed and added to the collective, definitely adds up and makes a difference.

Hopefully, this narrative, this collection of pieces, from individuals who care about you and our country, will inspire you to make the difference you all are entitled and required to make. I look forward to better days ahead and a better way. This day will be made for our kids, the future of America, by you and me.

We know what to do. . . .

Be Great!

MARCELLUS "DAT DUDE" WILEY is a graduate of Columbia University and former All-Pro Defensive End for the Jacksonville Jaguars, Dallas Cowboys, San Diego Chargers, and Buffalo Bills. He is now an ESPN TV analyst, as well as the founder of Wiley Enterprises and La'Tik Fashion Boutique. He is also the founder of the literacy-focused Marcellus Wiley Youth Foundation.

Dear Readers,

You've read the book. You've listened to us encourage, plead, and incite you to register to vote and go to the polls. Now what? Do you need specific information on how, when, and where to vote? Or maybe you're not yet old enough to vote, but you still want to get involved? Keep reading! There are many ways to declare yourself. The following is a list of suggestions to consider, resources to check out, and connections to make. Speak. Connect. Act. Vote. It's up to you.

*—A*MERICA *F*ERRERA

INVOLVE YOURSELF.

INFORM YOURSELF.

DECLARE YOURSELF.

HERE ARE SOME IDEAS TO GET YOU STARTED.

SPEAK

✪ Write a letter to the editor in response to an article or about any issue that's important to you. Your school paper, local newspaper, and national publications are always looking for new opinions. Many newspaper and magazine sites have feedback forms ready for you to type into directly. You're just a mouse click away from sending your message to the editors.

✪ Better yet, write your own article. Your best bet in having it seen will probably be with your school or local paper or in online forums, though you should still aim high. You might propose a point-counterpoint piece to a paper's editor, or just write something so strong that it will elicit responses all on its own.

✪ Speak out to an elected official—through a letter, on the phone, or in person. You, a constituent or future constituent of your mayor, representative, city council member, president, etc., are the voice these people want to hear. Talk about upcoming legislation that you support or oppose. Bring to light important issues that you feel have been ignored. Almost every elected official has his or her own website, featuring ways to get in touch. You are your elected officials' boss, so make sure they are living up to the job. Find your state and national representatives, as well as elections information, at **www.vote-smart.org**.

✪ Express your opinion at a school board or city hall meeting. Become involved in your school's organizations—student council, charity drives, and political groups—or start one of your own.

✪ Raise a sign at a rally. Raise your voice at a protest. Make a speech at a demonstration. Find out what's going on in your area by going to **www.meetup.com**.

✪ Use your virtual voice. Blog about a candidate or issue, make a statement on your profile page, or personalize your instant message profile.

Don't forget that speech can come in many forms. If you don't want to speak in public, think about creating art or music to make your statement. Wear a T-shirt that will get people talking. Make a bumper sticker that will stop traffic. Support someone or some group who says something you believe in.

Feed your brain and use your voice at these fantastic sites:

MySpace Impact Channel: This is a great resource for learning more about the candidates, connecting with organizations you might want to get involved with, and learning about young people and groups that have won awards for their community work. The site also features links to timely news articles, focuses on musicians and actors who have important messages to share, and even has an Impact Job Search, where you can find out about jobs or internships centered on making a difference. There are also lots of multimedia features, including music, videos, and more. **impact.myspace.com**

TakePart.com: This is a social action network where users can inspire, connect, and make a difference, using media as a resource and secret weapon. "Looking for groups, individuals or organizations to help create change or just to kick around ideas with? Here you go." **www.takepart.com**

Think MTV: This site has amazing overviews about key issues facing young people today, such as discrimination, education, the environment, global concerns, politics, and sexual health. Read timely articles about these topics and then find out how you can get involved directly through the site by creating or joining a "Think Group." You can also find your elected officials here simply by typing in your zip code. **www.mtv.com/thinkmtv**

Yahoo Elections: Features of this site include candidate profiles, the latest news, and an interactive Q&A feature where you can ask detailed questions about politics and government. Other notable aspects are links to election-related contests, a section of opinion articles from major newspapers, and interactive features such as online polls and candidate platform summaries. The site also offers great opportunities to connect with others and get involved. **elections.yahoo.com**

YouTube YouChoose '08: Get introduced to the candidates and find out where they stand on education, energy, health care, immigration, Iraq, the environment, and the economy. Post your own videos about the issues, and even direct a video question to a specific candidate. For the first time ever, videos of regular citizens' questions from the Internet are being shown to candidates at YouTube-sponsored debates, and these candidates are responding directly, taking this new medium very seriously. Watch videos of other citizens like you, watch videos of the candidates, and then make your own decision. Maybe make a video about why you've come to that decision to help influence your peers. Broadcast yourself! **www.youtube.com/youchoose**

Never underestimate the power you have in speaking to your friends, family members, and people in your community. Personal conversations often make the biggest impact—both in the "real world" and online. So, make the connection. . . .

Thanks in large part to the Internet, our generation is more connected than ever. We might meet in person and then touch

base online or vice versa, but once connected we will almost definitely stay connected mostly through an online community. So take advantage of this. If you're not sure how you want to get involved, think about making a connection online first.

But first you might want to know *who* you're connecting with:

CONNECT

Q: I hear people talk about young voters, but who does that mean exactly? I've heard us called "Generation Y," "Generation Next," and "the millennial generation." Who are we?

A: According to the NewsHour with Jim Lehrer and Pew Research Center, we are "the 42 million 16-to-25 year olds who watched the Twin Towers collapse, saw a student shoot down his peers at Virginia Tech University, grew up online and statistically speaking are better educated than any other generation in history." We are largely optimistic about the future and open-minded about a wide range of lifestyles and cultures, especially in comparison to older generations. This may be in large part because we as a group are very diverse—definitely more diverse than older voters. We are also realistic and thoughtful, and despite being on the whole happy to be living in the world today, we are also aware of many social problems, including among our peer group. We want to help change things. And since there's power in numbers, we definitely can: by 2015 we will make up one-third of eligible voters.

Q: How many of us are voting?

A: Despite what older people may think, today's youth are not so apathetic when it comes to voting and civic involvement. In 2004, 47% of 18-24–citizens voted. This added up to 11.6 million young voters—quite an increase from 2000's three million. In fact, this was the largest turnout of young voters since 1972. Even more notably, this increase in voting rate from the 2000 election was bigger than any other demographic's. 50% of eligible young women voted, and 44% of eligible young men did. A huge reason for this big increase in young voting was the record number of African Americans who voted.

In 2006 young people proved the skeptics wrong again by turning out in even greater numbers for the midterm election: two million *more* young voters came out to the polls as compared to the 2002 midterm elections. With such a great track record, and with four million eighteen-year-olds becoming eligible to vote in the upcoming election, all signs point to this generation's blowing everyone away with their turnout in 2008.

In the 2008 primaries that have been held as of this writing, virtually every state with comparable data from 2000 and 2004 has seen a significant increase in the number of young people who voted. And in even the one known exception so far, New York State, the youth vote held steady while older people there actually voted in smaller numbers than they had in the past.

Q: How are we voting?

A: In the 2006 midterm elections, more young people cast ballots for Democrats than Republicans across the board. For the House the rate was 58% versus 38%, in the Senate 60% to 33%, and 55% voted for Democratic governors over Republican ones (34%). However, many young people do not identify themselves as strictly Democrat or Republican. Though 18% of adults 30 and older strictly called themselves Independents, 26% of people younger than 30 did so.

According to the data available from 2008 thus far, young voters make up more of the Democratic electorate (about 14%) than they do the Republican (about 11%), though young voters of both parties have stepped it up and made their voices heard through their votes in the primaries, and independents are sure to follow suit when their candidates are on the ballot.

Now that we've met one another in theory, here are some ways we can connect in reality—even it's a virtual one:

✪ Find people and organizations who share the same goals and ideals as you and ask them about volunteer opportunities or forums for sharing your vision.

✪ Explore the websites of newspapers and organizations and connect with others who are giving feedback in the online forums and comments sections.

✪ Form a coalition of like-minded people and take action, or just adopt these people as a support group and sounding board.

✪ Connect by talking back and debating the issues—whether in a forum meant just for that or more casual spaces, like instant messaging, e-mail, and social networking pages. Blogs are also an easy and free way to start a dialogue with people around the world. Start one at **www.livejournal.com**.

✪ Start an e-mail petition or survey. Start a website. Start a movement.

✪ Start an interest group on Facebook, Friendster, or MySpace.

✪ Connect with political groups, nonprofit organizations, and political candidates by going to their websites, talking back, and getting involved.

---★---

While connecting online is a great thing, be careful about the personal information you give out, especially on your profile page. Since you can connect with almost anyone, likewise almost anyone can connect with you—whether or not you want them to or are even aware of it. So while it's great to get involved in lively debates, meet a community of people you would never meet in "real life," and make plans for some off-line activism, always maintain your privacy. Protect yourself and be smart. Some of the people you're connecting with online may not be who they claim to be.

Finally, be civil. Respect the people you're connecting with, even if you don't agree with them. Our forefathers gave us the right to vote and the right to free speech.

Speak and Connect totally overlap. So many of the Speak opportunities are also major opportunities to connect—and once you've connected, you can make the connection even stronger and bigger by organizing and acting, online and in the real world.

Here are some fantastic places to connect:

Alpha Kitties: "What's an Alpha Kitty, you ask? Someone who's brave, creative, fierce, passionate, and . . . well, yes, weird. Weird is the new normal, haven't you heard?" This is Atoosa Rubenstein's new movement to harness all these strong young people together and make a difference in the world. Find out how at **www.atoosa.com** and **www.youtube.com/AlphaKitty**.

Amber Tamblyn's official site: Unlike what you might expect from most actors, Amber Tamblyn's website is not just an excuse to toot her own horn. She reviews books and music, speaks out in her blog about things that are important to her, and gives visitors a massive message board to discuss anything and everything. Connect with this cool community at **www.amtam.com**.

Choose or Lose: An election website focused completely on voters your age. Find out the information that's critical to you. Hear what your peers have to say in youth-directed polls. And even after the election's over, add your two cents about the best way to move forward—whether your candidate won or lost. Don't miss out: **www.mtv.com/chooseorlose**.

The Freechild Project: "The mission of The Freechild Project is to advocate, inform, and celebrate social change led by and with young people around the world, particularly those who have been historically denied the right to participate." Their site hosts a youth issue database, a special resource collection, and project services to help groups working with young people. They've also got a compelling blog. Get started at **www.freechild.org**.

Generation Next Initiative: Embrace your power! First, watch the documentary that started it all. Then take advantage of the site's countless opportunities for you to talk back and connect, such as the Gen Next Dialogue and Op-Ed pieces in the Speak Up section and the kiosk videos in the Audio/Video section. There are also message boards and interactive news features. All at **www.pbs.org/newshour/generation-next.**

Norman Lear's official site: Norman Lear, the founder of Declare Yourself, has a really impressive résumé, including producing hit movies and TV shows. But perhaps the most amazing thing about him is all the work he's done to use his success and influence to help American democracy. Find out all about how he got the idea for Declare Yourself, his People For the American Way, and the very cool Norman Lear Center. Connect and get inspired at **www.normanlear.com**.

Social networking sites: You're already on Facebook, MySpace, and Friendster 24/7 anyway, so why not add some activism into your daily fun? For example, many organizations now have pages that you can connect to as their "friend," and many have widgets and logos that you can upload to your profile to show your support. To make things even easier, MySpace is an official media partner of Declare Yourself, which means that they've got direct links to voter registration tools as well as lots of multimedia information about the elections process. Go to **www.facebook.com, www.myspace.com, www.friendster.com,** and **www.declareyourself.com.**

The White House Project: "The White House Project is a non-partisan, nonprofit organization that aims to advance women's leadership in all communities and sectors—up to the U.S. presidency—by filling the leadership pipeline with a richly diverse, critical mass of women." A great cause to get involved with, no matter what your gender. Go to **www.thewhitehouseproject.org.**

Young Democrats of America: The YDA site has activist tools and resources, a blog, and information on how you can start your own chapter. The group represents Democrats under 36. **www.yda.org**. To connect with College Democrats of America, go to **www.collegedems.com**.

Young Republicans: Featuring useful links, resources, and information on events and campaigns, the site of the Young Republican National Federation is the place to connect with other members of the Republican Party aged 18–40. **www.yrnf.com**. You may also want to check out the College Republican National Committee at **www.crnc.org**.

Youth Noise: If you're under 27 and interested in connecting with others to discuss big issues and make a difference, this could be the social networking site for you. There are fourteen Cause Channels, with focuses ranging from Animal Rights to War & Peace, where you can find out more about the issues, get involved in a debate, and find related volunteer opportunities. Youth Noise also provides a forum to get others involved in your cause—by showing their support online *and* by showing up in real life to make an impact. **www.youthnoise.com**

★ ★ ★

Are you unhappy with the state of the world, the country, or the community around you? Do something about it. It's time to act!

ACT

✪ Draw up a survey or petition about an issue important to you, and use it to bring many voices together and make change.

✪ Intern or volunteer for a local elected official, state representative, congressperson, or even the president.

✪ Find an organization that does work you admire, and volunteer for it in the way you feel best utilizes your talents and passions. Or start your own project and recruit volunteers. Many organizations will even give young people grants to implement their projects. For ideas, see the list beginning on page 288.

✪ Have an alternative spring break. Whether you spend it on an organized service trip or do your own independent project, spring break is the perfect time to have fun *and* do something important. The memories may last even longer than those from an ordinary week at the beach . . . and the impact you can make definitely will. Check out Break Away at **www.alternativebreaks.org** or Habitat for Humanity at **www.habitat.org**.

✪ Volunteer abroad during the summer, or for a semester or school year. Or volunteer somewhere in the United States but far removed from your everyday life through an organization such as AmeriCorps or Teach For America.

✪ Run for office—at your school or in your town.

✪ Organize a beach or park cleanup, or run in a charity marathon with friends.

✪ Even if you're not yet eighteen, you can still be directly involved in the election process:

☞ Register others to vote. There are organizations dedicated solely to registering eligible voters, particularly people who might not have the right resources or knowledge of where and how to register, such as senior citizens, those of low socioeconomic status, new immigrants, and young people.

☞ Volunteer for an interest group or a particular candidate's campaign and be a part of *canvassing*. This might mean spreading the word about your candidate to potential constituents, fundraising, and/or conducting surveys and circulating petitions.

☞ Take others to vote. Many volunteer groups organize rides for people who cannot easily get to the polls. Get in touch with the office of a local political party or candidate, try an activist group or service organization like the United Way, or call a nursing home and offer your assistance directly.

☞ Volunteer to work at the polls on Election Day or during early voting and help count ballots. Many states allow and encourage students under eighteen to do this. Contact your county elections office to see how you can participate.

Here are some great organizations you might want to get involved with:

The American Cancer Society: "The American Cancer Society is at work in communities all across the country providing programs aimed at reducing the risk of cancer, detecting cancer as early as possible, ensuring proper treatment, and empowering people facing cancer to cope and maintain the highest possible quality of life." Get involved in areas such as education and awareness, patient service programs, advocacy, community events, and online volunteering. **www.cancer.org**

American Red Cross: "Red Cross volunteers provide relief to victims of disasters and help people prevent, prepare for, and respond to emergencies." You don't need any special skills to make such an important impact—the Red Cross will train you. **www.redcross.org**

The American Society for the Prevention of Cruelty to Animals: The ASPCA (or SPCA or Humane Society, as it may be known in your region) aims "to create a country of humane communities, one community at a time, where animals receive the compassion and respect they deserve—a nation where there is no more unnecessary euthanasia of adoptable animals simply because of a lack of resources and awareness." Along with political activism and local volunteer opportunities, you can also download an ASPCA fundraising widget for your blog or profile page. **www.aspca.org**

Amnesty International: "Amnesty International is a worldwide movement of people who campaign for internationally recognized human rights for all." Get involved in your local chapter, or start one of your own. **www.amnesty.org**

Big Brothers Big Sisters: Become a Big Brother or Big Sister. "Big Brothers Big Sisters mentors children, ages 6 through 18, in communities across the country. The Big Brothers Big Sisters Mission is to help children reach their potential through professionally supported, one-to-one relationships with mentors that have a measurable impact on youth." **www.bbbs.org**

The Campus Climate Challenge: Involve your school. "The Campus Climate Challenge is a project of more than 30 leading youth organizations throughout the U.S. and Canada. The Challenge leverages the power of young people to organize on college campuses and high schools across Canada and the U.S. to win 100% Clean Energy policies at their schools." **www.campusclimatechallenge.org**

Declare Your School: Start your own voter registration drive! Declare Yourself offers an easy step-by-step guide to holding your own voter registration drive on campus or in your neighborhood. They even offer printable materials for your table. **www.DeclareYourself.com/voting_faq/declare_your_school.html**

The Genocide Intervention Fund: "The Genocide Intervention Network envisions a world in which the global community is willing and able to protect civilians from genocide and mass atrocities." Its mission: "to empower individuals and communities with the tools to prevent and stop genocide." Help to stop the genocide in Darfur—and around the world—by challenging the candidates, becoming a part of the Student Anti-Genocide Coalition, or joining the Sudan Divestment Task Force. **www.genocideinterventionfund.org**

The Global AIDS Alliance: "The mission of the Global AIDS Alliance (GAA) is to galvanize the political will and financial resources needed to slow, and ultimately stop, the global AIDS crisis and reduce its impacts on poor countries hardest hit by the pandemic." Help break down the stigma attached to HIV and AIDS by educating yourself and others and find local opportunities to do this through **www.globalaidsalliance.org.**

The Human Rights Campaign: "The Human Rights Campaign is America's largest civil rights organization working to achieve gay, lesbian, bisexual and transgender equality." Attend an event, participate in HRC's online advocacy center, and educate others. **www.hrc.org**

Human Rights Watch: Human Rights Watch is a U.S.-based organization that focuses on researching and conducting investigations on human rights abuses around the world as well as locally. Their HRW Young Advocates group is made up of young professionals who "conduct research, educate the community and advocate change." This is a great way to get active! **www.hrw.org/community**

LIFEBeat: Aimed at educating young people, "LIFEbeat mobilizes the talents and resources of the music industry to raise awareness . . . and to provide support to the AIDS community." Are you an artist or musician? You can help out by participating in their Outreach or Hearts and Voices programs. Or get the Do It Yourself Kit to learn how to start an awareness campaign at your school. **www.lifebeat.org**

The National Conference for Community and Justice: NCCJ "is a human relations organization dedicated to fighting bias, bigotry and racism in America." Volunteer positions include fund-raisers, designers, camp counselors, event staff, and more. **www.nccj.org**

Our Education: A nonprofit created by college students, "Our Education is the voice of young people across the country who believe that all American children should have access to high quality education." Sign the national student petition, take part in the Student Voice Project, and spread the word by becoming a petition drive director at your school. **www.oured.org**

Peace Corps: "Peace Corps Volunteers work in the following areas: education, youth outreach, and community development; business development; agriculture and environment; health and HIV/AIDS; and information technology." If you're a college graduate, the Peace Corps is an unparalleled opportunity for hands-on immersion in another culture while you volunteer to better our global society. **www.peacecorps.gov**

The ONE Campaign: "ONE is Americans of all beliefs and every walk of life—united as ONE—to help make poverty history." The site tells you how you can lobby Congress, volunteer at the local level, and join an online community to be a part of organizing. Especially noteworthy: their ONE Vote '08 campaign, a nonpartisan movement to make global disease and extreme poverty major priorities in the 2008 election. **www.one.org**

The Sierra Club: This environmental group organizes political actions, such as petitions and lobbying, on a national level, and there are also regional groups you can join to take direct action at a local level. "When you join or give to the Sierra Club you will have the satisfaction of knowing that you are helping to preserve irreplaceable wildlands, save endangered and threatened wildlife, and protect this fragile environment we call home." **www.sierraclub.org**

Teach For America: "Teach For America is the national corps of outstanding recent college graduates . . . of all academic majors . . . who commit two years to teach in urban and rural public schools and become leaders in the effort to expand educational opportunity." You don't have to be an education major to be part of this elite group, and in fact, a diversity of majors are welcomed and needed. **www.teachforamerica.org**

UNICEF (The United Nations International Children's Emergency Fund): "UNICEF is the driving force that helps build a world where the rights of every child are realized. We have the global authority to influence decision-makers, and the variety of partners at grassroots level to turn the most innovative ideas into reality." Among the many worthy causes you can learn about and support here is the Unite for Children Unite Against AIDS campaign. You can also become part of Voices of Youth, a worldwide forum of young people connecting to come up with ways to better the world. **www.unicef.org**

YMCA: "Despite its name, the YMCA is not just for the young, not just for men, and not just for Christians." In fact, it is "an association of members who come together with a common understanding of the YMCA mission and a common commitment to the YMCA's vision of building strong kids, strong families and strong communities." There are countless opportunities to get involved at your local Y, ranging from coaching a team to serving on a committee. **www.ymca.net**

Young People For: "Young People For (YP4) is a long-term leadership development program that identifies, engages, and empowers progressive leaders to promote social change in their communities." Apply for a YP4 fellowship and get support—including financial assistance, career development, and networking—for your goals for your campus or community. And you'll kick it all off with a paid trip to the National Summit in Washington, DC, where you'll connect with other young leaders. "What do you stand for?" **www.youngpeoplefor.org**

Or if you're not quite sure what issue you want to focus on, start your research here. These sites can tell you about volunteer opportunities of all types:

AmeriCorps: "Each year, AmeriCorps offers 75,000 opportunities for adults of all ages and backgrounds to serve through a network of partnerships with local and national nonprofit groups." Completion of your project can also earn you money for college. AmeriCorps is part of the Corporation for National and Community Service (**www.nationalservice.gov**), another clearinghouse for information on volunteering. **www.AmeriCorps.org**

Boost Mobile RockCorps: Boost Mobile RockCorps "encourages volunteerism in young people. It was created to effect social change and act as a bridge between communities in need and the young people who want to make them better." You can also get free concert tickets when you volunteer through this organization. **www.boostmobilerockcorps.org**

Do Something: "You have a lot of ideas about how you'd like to change the world or at least you have a lot of questions and concerns and you're looking for specific things you can do. We're giving you a place to connect, a place to be inspired, be supported, be celebrated." Specifically for teens, this site also features grant and scholarship opportunities, message boards, and profiles of Do Something Clubs across the nation. Start one at your school. **www.dosomething.org**

State Public Interest Research Groups (PIRGs): "The state PIRGs are independent, state-based, citizen-funded organizations that advocate for the public interest." If you're interested in grassroots activism such as canvassing, this is the site for you. Find your state or campus PIRG's website and get mobilized. **www.pirg.org** and **www.studentpirgs.org**

United Way: "In communities across America, 1350 United Ways improve lives by mobilizing the caring power of their communities." The United Way brings together an astounding array of groups and volunteer opportunities, and the only problem may be deciding between them. **www.unitedway.org**

VolunteerMatch: "Want to start volunteering? There are hundreds of ways to help out. With VolunteerMatch, it's never been easier to find a rewarding way to give back and make a difference." With more than 30,000 nonprofit organizations linked to the site, you're sure to find the right fit. **www.volunteermatch.org**

Youth Service America: "Youth Service America is a resource center that partners with thousands of organizations committed to increasing the quality and quantity of volunteer opportunities for young people, ages 5–25, to serve locally, nationally, and globally." Along with many organized service days to be a part of, YSA offers grants to students with inspiration to change the world but lacking the money to do so. **www.ysa.org**

Youth Venture: "Youth Venture inspires and invests in teams of young people to design and launch their own lasting social ventures, enabling them to have this transformative experience of leading positive social change." Have an amazing idea but not sure how to go about implementing it? Youth Venture will help you dream it, do it, and grow it. **www.youthventure.org**

★　★　★

VOTE!

Who can vote:

If you are a United States citizen eighteen or older, you are eligible to vote. (Many states require a voter be eighteen at least thirty days before an election, and have restrictions on voting by prisoners, ex-felons, and the mentally incompetent. You can find out the requirements for your state along with many other Voting FAQs at **www.declareyourself.com**.)

How to register:

There are many opportunities to register to vote. Voter registration cards can be found at schools, libraries, community centers, and driver's license centers. You may also see them at public gatherings such as college events and concerts. But perhaps the most convenient way to register is online. **Declareyourself.com** makes it easy: you just click to download a form and then mail it to the address provided for your state. The registration form is simple. The site also tells you state-specific information, such as deadlines and ID requirements. Most states require voters to register at least thirty days before an election, so don't put it off until the last minute or you may miss your first chance to make your vote count.

Some states may ask you to designate your political party on your voter registration, but you are not required to choose one if you don't want to. Just know that in states with closed primaries, only those voters registered as being part of the party can vote in their primary. Other states have open primaries, in which your stated allegiance—or lack of any party affiliation at all—does not prohibit you from being eligible to vote in a party primary.

Voting while away from home:

You must be a resident of the state and county where you're registered to be able to vote there. If you're away at school and an official resident of the county your college is in, you can register and vote there. However, if your permanent address (the one listed on your ID) is still your hometown, then you may want to vote as an absentee. Once you've registered to vote in your hometown's district and received confirmation of your registration, request an absentee ballot from your state's elections office—you'll need to ask for a new one for each upcoming election. Some states make the process even easier by allowing you to make your request online. A few weeks before the official Election Day, you'll get a paper ballot, which you send back to your hometown's elections office by the date they tell you. Most states offer absentee voting, but they all operate a bit differently, so make sure you find out the deal for your situation.

Members of the military and American citizens living in other countries also have the right to vote as absentees. The rules are slightly different than those for citizens currently in the United States, so the Federal Voting Assistance Program is there to help at **www.fvap.gov**.

Reregistering:

If you have made your permanent residency in a new place, then you need to register to vote there. Every time you change your official address, you should let your local election official know by sending a letter or by filling out a new voter registration form with your current information. Even if you stay in the same state and county, your voting precinct could change, so it's important to update the information. Local elections and polling places are dependent on your address. Remember: you can only be registered to vote in one place at once and can only participate in an election held by your current, most recent voting precinct.

Early voting:

Many states allow registered voters to vote early, allocating an alternate day (often several) during which voters can go to the polls when it's best for their schedules. This is a great thing to take advantage of so you can be sure that your vote will get counted and not have to worry about something unforeseen that may come up on Election Day itself. Often polls will be open on weekends and at many convenient locations. Some states have early voting in person while others allow mail-in ballots. Find out if your state allows early voting by visiting your state's election website.

Find out where your polling place is:
Polling places and times will be listed in the local newspaper and will also be on your state's elections office website.

What to bring:
Though not all states require it, it's a good idea to bring your ID. It's also wise to bring your voter registration confirmation—and some states require it, especially those that call it a "voter ID." In most states you're also allowed to bring any literature or notes you might have to help you remember who and what you plan to vote for.

It is important to keep in mind that every state is a little bit different when it comes to voting rules, procedures, and deadlines. DeclareYourself.com is a great place to find out about your specific state, as well as to get all your voting questions answered. The site has links to every state's elections office website—where you can register to vote, find about absentee and early voting, and determine your polling place.

INFORM YOURSELF

Don't just let anyone tell you what to think! Find out all you can about the issues and candidates and make your own informed decisions. The following resources can help you do this, and are the perfect starting point for speaking and connecting:

By the People: An educational site with features such as election-related history, an election glossary, tips on how to be a Savvy Voter, and opinion articles. There are also links to other helpful sites. **www.pbs.org/elections**

Close Up Foundation's First Vote 2008: This initiative is a free program aimed at schools that provides information and tools to follow the election and conduct your own mock presidential election, thus educating first-time voters through the activities and resources found on their website. The program also hopes to inspire teachers to focus at least one full class to the topic of voting and to make it easy for their students to register to vote. If your school is not yet involved, ask your social studies or government teacher if your class can be a part of the program. **www.closeup.org/frstvote.htm**

Comedy Central's Address the Mess: There's nothing funny about an ailing environment, but that doesn't mean you can't have fun working to save it. This campaign "is committed to showing viewers easy ways to reduce waste, improve their lives and help revive the planet." Get environmental tips, watch hilarious-while-helpful videos, and take a quiz on how environmentally savvy you are—and how you can become even more so. **www.addressthemess.com**

Democracy Now!: Are you cynical about media sources who have to answer to advertisers and who often seem to be more focused on entertainment value and profit than on facts? Democracy Now! is a great alternative, a completely independently run news program that gets its stories from independent and international journalists. **www.democracynow.org**

The Democracy Project: This gives a really basic overview of some important aspects of American democracy, with topics such as "How does government affect me?" "Be president for a day," and "Step inside the voting booth." Even though it was designed for young kids, it's a great starting point, especially for its "virtual tours." **www.pbskids.org/democracy**

Governmental sites: Go straight to the source! Look up proposed bills, find out more about your elected representatives, and find all the answers to questions you may have about how our democratic system works. Bring history to life by reading and searching the Constitution and Declaration of Independence. There are also opportunities here to communicate directly with representatives. Connect to: the White House (**www.whitehouse.gov**), United States House of Representatives (**www.house.gov**), United States Senate (**www.senate.gov**), United States Supreme Court (**www.supremecourtus.gov**), United States National Archives and Records Administration (**www.archives.gov;** this is an especially good place to learn about elections and get an overview of the United States Electoral College), and the Library of Congress (**www.loc.gov,** especially **www.loc.gov.learn/features/election**).

The League of Women Voters: Despite the name, this organization is not just for women. "The League of Women Voters, a nonpartisan political organization, has fought since 1920 to improve our systems of government and impact public policies through citizen education and advocacy. The League is a grassroots organization, working at the national, state and local levels." This group is a wonderful resource for information on the candidates in your area. In addition to the information found on their website, each local chapter publishes comprehensive guides on the candidates so that you can make an informed decision. They are also a great group to volunteer for if you care about voting rights and government accountability. **www.lwv.org**

National Public Radio: "NPR (National Public Radio) is an internationally acclaimed producer and distributor of noncommercial news, talk, and entertainment programming." Find your local NPR station and listen to it on the radio or online and get in-depth perspective on the issues, without interruptions by advertisers. You'll learn about comprehensive national and international news, as well as local issues. **www.npr.org**

On the Media: When you find yourself wondering how to deal with the conflicting information you might be hearing from various news sources, or if you want to make sure you're thinking critically about things and not being influenced by slick, savvy media manipulation, check out On the Media. Airing on NPR, "On the Media explores how the media 'sausage' is made, casts an incisive eye on fluctuations in the marketplace of ideas, and examines threats to the freedom of information and expression in America and abroad. For one hour a week, the show tries to lift the veil from the process of 'making media,' especially news media, because it's through that lens that we literally see the world and the world sees us." **www.onthemedia.org**

Young Voter Strategies: This research organization focuses on young voters and how to energize them to be involved in all elections. Their website is a fantastic source of statistics, campaign toolkits, and news, all focused on the "Millennial Generation": you! **www.youngvoterstrategies.org**

And many more: The more research you do, the more informed you will be. Ultimately the decisions you make are up to you, and you may decide to choose one news source to depend on, which is a perfectly good strategy. To reach this decision, you may want to start with a nonprofit, nonpartisan group like the **Center for Voting and Democracy (www.fairvote.org)**, **Project Vote Smart (www.vote-smart.org)**, or **Public Agenda (www.public agenda.org)** and then work from there. These sites can be great jumping-off points to connect you to research organizations that focus specifically on the issues important to you.

And don't forget about **Declare Yourself!** In many ways this is your one-stop shop for all your voting and elections needs. With links to news sources (including **UWire, www.uwire.com**, a roundup of the best student-produced news nationwide), media partners, voter registration info, statistics, and loads of fun videos and photos, this is an ideal launching pad for getting informed and involved. Find it all at **www.declareyourself.com**.

Timeline of Voting Rights in America

1776: The Declaration of Independence is drafted and signed. Declare Yourself has quite the connection to the Declaration, as Norman Lear (founder of Declare Yourself) purchased a rare broadside copy of the Declaration that now travels the country. To find out if the Declaration is coming to a town near you, go here: **www.declareyourself.com/about_us/about_us_6.html**.

1789: The United States Constitution takes effect. It gives states the power to decide to whom they will grant voting rights. The states largely make restrictions based on land ownership (which, in turn, limited voting to a small elite class of white men). Article II of the Constitution also established in principle the United States Electoral College, stating that for presidential elections each state will have electors who will represent their states' populations.

1804: The Twelfth Amendment to the Constitution is passed. This clarifies that members of the Electoral College must cast separate ballots for president and vice president, so as to avoid the confusion and conflicts not doing so had caused in previous elections.

1848: The Seneca Falls Convention is the first women's rights convention in the United States. Held in Seneca Falls, New York, and led by Elizabeth Cady Stanton and Lucretia Mott, this is considered the start of the Women's Suffrage Movement in the United States.

1856: By this time, the majority of white men in the United States have the right to vote.

1865: The Thirteenth Amendment to the Constitution is enacted, abolishing slavery.

1868: The Fourteenth Amendment to the Constitution takes effect, stating that all natural-born or naturalized citizens have equal citizenship rights under the law, and no state can impinge upon this. This established the principles of equal protection under the law and due process of the law.

1870: The Fifteenth Amendment to the Constitution is ratified, stating that race, color, or previous slave status cannot be used as reasons to keep a citizen from voting.

Late 1870s–1965: Despite the aforementioned laws, many African Americans and other minorities continue to be denied their equal rights under the law. Many states enforce **discriminatory Jim Crow laws**, which they claim, in order to appear to be abiding by federal law, give "separate but equal" treatment to nonwhites. In actuality, the treatment was not at all equal, and often included systematic and illegal intimidation at the polls as well as discriminatory barriers to voting, such as poll taxes and literacy tests.

1913–1917: By 1913 ten states have **granted women the right to vote**, beginning with Wyoming in 1869. But **women are still fighting for the right to be granted nationwide,** and many are arrested and even thrown in jail for being involved in protests and civil disobedience.

1920: The Nineteenth Amendment to the Constitution passes, granting women the right to vote.

1946–1956 and 1961–1965: African-American civil rights groups organize large-scale voter registration drives as part of the American civil rights movement.

1951: The Twenty-second Amendment to the Constitution establishes that a United States president can only serve two four-year terms.

1964: The Civil Rights Act of 1964 declares that "separate but equal" is unconstitutional, and outlaws segregation in public places, notably schools, public transportation, and places of business. It outlaws discrimination based on race or sex in employment and housing practices and establishes the Equal Employment Opportunity Commission. Therefore, women are also greatly helped by this law.

1964: The Twenty-fourth Amendment to the Constitution bans both state and federal governments from having any kind of poll tax used as a criterion for voting eligibility.

1965: The Voting Rights Act of 1965 is signed into law, finally and truly establishing universal suffrage in the United States. Among other protections to encourage minority voting and outlaw all further discrimination against minorities at the polls, it bans any kind of literacy test as a prerequisite for voting in all federal, state, and local elections.

1971: The Twenty-sixth Amendment to the Constitution rules that citizens aged eighteen and up have the right to vote in all United States elections, no matter for what level of government. Before this, many states limited voting to twenty-one and up.

1975: The Voting Rights Act is amended to explicitly extend its protections to Asian, Hispanic, and Native American citizens, by requiring that bilingual ballots and translators are available for those who need them.

1993: The Voter Registration Act was signed into law in 1993, and officially took effect in 1995, requiring that state governments make it easier for people to register to vote, offering clear, uniform voter registration forms at places like schools, libraries, and driver's license renewal centers. For this reason, the law is sometimes referred to as "Motor Voter."

2002: The Help America Vote Act was created largely because of the controversy over uncounted or incorrectly counted votes in the highly contested 2000 presidential election. It requires states to reassess and update their voting systems and procedures, and it allocates funds to help the states do so.

GLOSSARY OF ELECTION-RELATED TERMS

administration: The word *administration* is used to talk about the office that a government official heads and its policies. It is most often used to refer to the office of president. A president's administration includes his or her cabinet, who are the highest appointed officials chosen to coserve in the executive branch. *See also: separation of powers.*

campaign: A political campaign comprises the processes, events, and efforts by which candidates seek to gain support from voters to elect them to a specific office, or by an interest group attempting to pass or defeat a certain proposition up for a vote. *See also: administration, constituents, electorate, referendum.*

canvassing: Canvassing is when a group of people organize to target a certain region or group of people. In regard to elections, canvassers from issue-focused organizations (such as nonprofits, churches, and political parties) or from candidates' campaigns themselves will contact people systematically to fund-raise, encourage them to vote for a particular candidate, or even just to register to vote. A canvass can be done through door-to-door interactions, on the phone, or by approaching people in public places.

caucus: A caucus is a meeting held to discuss issues and ideals and then to make action-focused decisions based on that discussion. You hear the word *caucus* used most often during the United States presidential campaigns in reference to electing presidential candidates. While people in most states vote in primaries for whom they'd like to be the presidential candidate, Iowans in particular do things a bit differently. They hold caucuses with fellow precinct members to discuss issues that are important to them, propose party platforms, and decide whom they would like to represent them at the party's regional, state, and national conventions. There are no official elections at the caucuses, but instead caucus attendees nominate these delegates who will vote on their behalf. For more than thirty years, the Iowa caucus has been the first major event in the American presidential campaign, and therefore Iowa is a hot stop for presidential hopefuls of both parties, who come to woo and impress the voters in hopes of winning their support. Sometimes the terms caucus and primary are used interchangeably, but most states' so-called caucuses have the structure of a primary. Caucuses are also held among groups of elected officials, such as congressional caucuses, to decide on issues and advance certain interests. *See also: delegate, political party, primary election, voting precinct.*

constituents: An elected official's constituents are the people he or she represents—or is campaigning to represent. Often used interchangeably with *constituents*, the word constituency refers to these potential voters' as a region or a whole. State legislators determine the boundaries of electoral districts for United States congressional representation. When these districts are changed, it is called redistricting or reapportionment. Redistricting can be controversial, as some redistricting can be perceived to be for strategic partisan gain. This is known as gerrymandering. In cases of extreme controversy, such as alleged discrimination, the judicial branch intervenes. *See also: campaign, electorate.*

delegate: A delegate is a member of a group chosen to represent all its members, and to make decisions and cast votes in the best interests of the group. In American politics the term is often used in reference to political party delegates, who represent each state at the party's national convention and usually are pledged to vote at the convention for the presidential candidate his or her constituency has chosen in a caucus or primary. *See also: caucus, political party, primary, superdelegates, United States Congress.*

Election Day: National (or Federal) elections in the United States are always held on the Tuesday after the first Monday in November. Elections for president are held every four years, and elections for the House and Senate are held every two years. Those elections that don't include a presidential election are called midterm elections. Many state and local elections are also held on this date for convenience's sake, but this is not required. Additionally, several states allow early voting, which means that people are allowed to vote on a day or series of days prior to the election, giving an alternate option to people who may be unavailable on voting day. Finally, a majority of states allow absentee voting, which allows voters to cast their ballots by mail if they will not be in their voting precinct on Election Day. *See also: primary election.*

electorate: All the citizens who are eligible to vote in an election make up the electorate. *See also: constituents.*

incumbent: The incumbent is the person who currently occupies a political position. When running for reelection against a new candidate, the incumbent is often considered or assumed to have the advantage. If this person is leading in the polls, he or she is called the front-runner. *See also: polls/polling place, term limits.*

local, city, and state elections: Equally as important as federal elections, if not more so, these are the times you vote for members of the school board, mayor, city council members, governor, and other state and local representatives. It is also a time to make your voice heard on important local issues and proposals outlined in referenda (or referendums). It is important to note that, unlike in the electing of the president, your popular vote *directly* decides the outcome of these elections, just as it does in midterm elections.

Depending on your state's laws, you may or may not elect some officials such as judges. In some places, such positions are appointed. *See also: referendum.*

majority and minority leaders: The majority and minority leaders are Congress members selected by their parties to be official coordinators for their respective parties in the Senate and House of Representatives, and to promote party goals and ideals. They are also called floor leaders, and work alongside the whips. *See also: two-party system, United States Congress, whips.*

partisan, partisanship: The term *partisan* is used to describe a person or issue strongly associated with a single party or political viewpoint. When something is done in collaboration of the two parties, or without regard to specific party interests, it is called *bipartisan*, or *nonpartisan*. *See also: political party, two-party system.*

plurality voting system: The United States Electoral College largely operates by a plurality system for our presidential elections, in which "the winner takes all." In other words, the majority of the popular vote—even if it's only 51%—decides to whom all one state's electoral votes will go. This system has been criticized because of the perception that the people who voted for the less popular candidate in a state do not get a direct voice at the national level. *See also: two-party system, United States Electoral College.*

political party: A political party is a group of people with similar viewpoints on government and law, who unite to promote like-minded candidates for elected office. A party platform is such a group's stated stance on important, high-profile issues, that a party's candidate is expected to represent and promote if elected. Political parties announce their presidential platforms at national conventions, which are generally held in the late summer or early fall of election year. These conventions bring together party delegates from every state, who officially nominate and announce their party's presidential candidate. *See also: delegate, Election Day, partisan, two-party system.*

polls/polling place: Your polling place or station is the designated location in your voting precinct where you will cast your ballot. It will likely be in a school, library, firehouse, or other public venue. Going to your polling place to cast your ballot is also referred to as "going to the polls."

The word *poll* can also mean a survey, such as those measuring a president's approval rating or asking people for whom they *plan* to vote. These are opinion polls, which are pulled together by pollsters, who contact people by phone, mail, e-mail, or in person to try to gauge public attitudes on various topics or to try to predict election outcomes. These pollsters may be working for news media, universities, nonprofit groups, or the candidates themselves. Informal polls conducted at organized events like caucuses or a school student council meeting are called straw polls.

Finally, an exit poll is when you have just finished voting and a pollster asks if you wouldn't mind sharing for whom you voted. You have no obligation to answer, of course, since your vote is anonymous and confidential. But if you do provide them with the information, they will use it to predict the winner before the official results come in. These pollsters generally work for the news media, and they look especially for demographic information—such as your age, gender, race, and socioeconomic status—to analyze what kind of people voted for each candidate. Of course there would be no way to ask everyone coming out of the voting booth, so pollsters interview a very small fraction of exiting voters in hopes of getting a representative sample of the general population that will allow them to make broader predictions and analyses of the country at large.

popular vote: The word *popular* literally means "of the people," and that's exactly what the popular vote is: it's the votes cast by individuals like you. For United States presidential elections, the popular vote is important at the state level, since most states' popular majority determines which way its electoral votes will go. *See also: plurality voting system, United States Electoral College.*

presidential succession: The line of presidential succession determines who will succeed (come next) to the position if the president no longer can, for whatever reason, act as the head of state. This person will be the acting (or temporary) president until a new election can take place or the elected president can resume his or her office, depending on the circumstance. Likewise, if the next highest ranking person is unavailable, the succession moves on to the next in line. In the United States, as established by the Presidential Succession Act of 1947, the vice president is first in line, followed by the speaker of the House, the president of the Senate *pro tempore*, and then the secretary of state, all the way down through the president's cabinet. It should be noted that even an acting president has to fulfill the presidential eligibility requirements set forth in the Constitution. Thus those in line who are younger than thirty-five years old and/or not natural-born United States citizens will be skipped over.

president of the Senate *ex officio* and *pro tempore*: The vice president of the United States is, "by right of office," also president of the Senate: the position is given to him or her as part of his holding the vice-presidential office. Although the role is largely symbolic, and the vice president does not generally preside over the Senate, he or she does have a tiebreaking vote.

Pro tempore means "for the time being," and so the president of the Senate *pro tempore* is the highest ranking person in the Senate when the United States vice president is absent. He or she is generally the highest ranking senator of the majority party and has been elected by his or her fellow senators. This position, depending on the particular attitude of the officeholder, is generally more an honor than an active job; part of the role entails being the Senate's representative at official functions. However, the officeholder does have some important powers, such as signing off on legislation before it goes to the president and ruling on Senate procedure. *See also: presidential succession, Speaker of the House of Representatives, two-party system, United States Congress.*

primary election, primary: While primaries also take place at the local level, in national conversation the primary most often referenced is the election where people vote for whom they would like to represent them at their party convention and/or whom they would like to be their party's presidential candidate, depending on the state. The general election is the actual election of the president, done on Election Day. A closed primary is open only to voters from a particular party, whereas an open primary allows any voter to participate. Whether a primary is open or closed depends on the state. By New Hampshire law, the first primary in the presidential election is always the New Hampshire primary, and it is generally held shortly after the Iowa caucus. Like the Iowa caucus, the New Hampshire primary draws a lot of attention from each party's candidates and the media. Hoping to get similar treatment, many other states have started moving their primaries and caucuses earlier and earlier, causing New Hampshire to move theirs even earlier to still be first, garnering some criticism. Some say that this schedule draws out the expensive, media-heavy presidential campaigns unnecessarily. This trend has also been criticized out of concern that it will lead to a focus on only certain states' wants and needs, which may not represent the diversity of the country. *See also: caucus, Election Day.*

referendum: Allowed by many state and local governments, a referendum (plural: *referenda* or *referendums*) sets forth a proposal and allows the electorate to vote on it directly. Some examples of what a referendum might be about include: whether to allocate local tax dollars to be used to fund the construction of a sports arena, proposing an amendment to the state constitution regarding gay marriage, or deciding whether or not to keep a city's affirmative action law. Referenda are also referred to as propositions, initiatives, legislative referrals, and ballot measures. Since referenda bypass the usual legislative process of lawmaking, they are an example of direct democracy. *See also: electorate; local, city, and state elections; representative democracy.*

representative democracy: The United States is a representative democracy, which means that we elect officials to represent us and make decisions on law and policy, hopefully in the best interests of their constituency. If a representative's constituents decide that he or she is no longer representing them as promised or expected, they have the opportunity to elect someone else when a term is up, and a new election takes place. In contrast to representative democracy, direct democracy involves individual citizens voting directly on proposals and issues. *See also: constituents, referendum.*

separation of powers: The United States Constitution set forth a separation of powers between the executive branch, the legislative branch, and the judicial branch, so that there would always be checks and balances to avoid one branch dominating every aspect of government. In the national government, the executive branch is the president and his or her cabinet members. The executive branch's role officially is to enforce laws and oversee the running of the country, while the legislative branch makes laws, and the judicial branch interprets them. Similar separations of powers exist at state and local levels as well. *See also: administration.*

Speaker of the House of Representatives: The speaker of the House is the highest ranking person in the United States House of Representatives and the head of the majority party in Congress. Speakers are elected by their political party, and come into power when that party gains majority. The Speaker's role is generally more active than that of the president of the Senate *pro tempore,* but there are similarities in the official procedural and symbolic duties involved in both positions. He or she presides over almost every joint session but often passes down the overseeing of everyday House discussions to other party members. *See also: presidential succession, president of the Senate, two-party system, United States Congress.*

suffrage: Suffrage means the right to vote, from the Latin word for "vote." The vote can also be called political franchise or enfranchisement, which comes from the old-fashioned phrase "to grant a franchise to," meaning to grant someone citizenship and all the rights that come with it, as well as to free them from slavery. Those who are restricted from voting in any way are called disenfranchised.

Those who fought for women's right to vote were often referred to as suffragists or suffragettes. The women's suffrage movement in the United States finally achieved victory in 1920. In theory, the Nineteenth Amendment finally granted universal suffrage: voting rights to all adults regardless of race, religious belief, former slave status, intelligence, education, socioeconomic status, or gender. However, many African Americans were still being disenfranchised in this country under Jim Crow laws. As part of the widespread discrimination enforced under these racist state and local laws, many state governments did everything they could to prevent African Americans and other minorities from voting, including a requirement of would-be voters to pay poll taxes and/or pass literacy tests (which they unconstitutionally waived or rigged in favor of most whites). These remaining discriminatory laws were finally abolished under the Civil Rights Act of 1964 and the Voting Rights Act of 1965.

But the idea that an eighteen-year-old was to be considered a voting adult was not officially established until the Twenty-sixth Amendment was passed in 1971. Today all adults citizens eighteen and up have the right to vote, with the exception, in most states, of prisoners. Some states also restrict ex-prisoners from voting, particularly felons.

superdelegate: In contrast to the normal "pledged" delegates, who represent each state at the party's national convention and have agreed to vote for a certain candidate based on the popular vote of a primary or caucus (though in rare cases they do switch their vote), the Democratic party also has *superdelegates*. These are "unpledged" representatives who also vote for the Democratic presidential candidate at the nominating convention, and they make up almost 20% of the total delegate count. These powerful people—mostly current or former elected officials, as well as Democratic National Committee members—automatically get voting rights at the party convention. In a tight race for the nomination, when neither candidate has the plurality of delegate votes required to be declared the winner, the superdelegates can be the ones to cast the deciding ballots. And the suspense can remain tense up until the final vote at the convention, as the superdelegates' unpledged status means they are not bound to vote for one candidate or the other or to reveal who they plan to vote for in advance, though some do share this information. While the Republican Party also has some party officials who automatically vote at their nominating convention, the informal term "superdelegate," as well as this larger system, is unique to the Democratic Party. *See also: delegates, political party.*

swing state: A swing state is one in which there is no clear majority for one presidential candidate or the other, and so that state's Electoral College votes could go either way. For this reason, presidential candidates often concentrate a lot of time and attention on these states, in hopes that they can get these swing voters to vote for them. *See also: United States Electoral College.*

term limits: Term limits are restrictions on the length of time an elected official can serve in his or her position. The *term* is the initial amount of time a person is elected to serve, and the limit is placed on the number of times this term can be repeated, if at all. Sometimes the limit is placed on the total number of terms, period, while sometimes it simply limits the number of terms a person can serve in a row.

As set forth in the Twenty-second Amendment of the Constitution (ratified in 1951), no United States president can serve more than two four-year terms. There are currently no term limits in the United States House or Senate, although there have been constitutional amendments proposed to change this. A

House term is two years, and a Senate term is six years, but they can be repeated for as long as that member is reelected.

two-party system: While other parties are welcome and active in the American political scene, the United States has historically been largely a two-party system. This means that two major political parties, the Democratic Party and the Republican Party, tend to dominate elections and their resulting government administrations. The party that has the majority in the House of Representatives and/or in the Senate is called the majority party, and the other is called the minority party. Often as a reaction to an administration dominated by one party, midterm elections will result in the other party gaining power in the legislature, ostensibly because the electorate is unhappy with the dominant party's actions and they wish to balance things out and/or change things.

It is notable that many other of the world's representative democracies are not dominated by two parties. Many countries in Europe, for example, have coalition governments in which several parties receive significant shares of the votes—none able to get a majority—and so the different representatives have to work together to make all voters happy. A likely reason that such governments don't result in the United States, at least nationally, is because of the plurality voting system that we have in the United States based on our Electoral College. Many other countries have proportional representation, in which the popular vote more directly affects the election.

In the United States, there are dozens of official third parties or minor parties, including the Green Party, the Libertarian Party, the Constitution Party, and the Working Families Party. Candidates can also run as independents, but this can become difficult, as most states require evidence of a certain amount of voter support in a previous election to get officially on a state ballot. If your voter registration form asks you for a political party and you do not want to choose one or you feel that your views are not represented by any of the parties listed, you can also list your status as "independent." However, depending on your state, whether or not you are registered as being part of a party may affect your eligibility to vote in primary elections. *See also: Election Day, partisan, political party, plurality voting system, primary election, United States Electoral College.*

United States Congress: The United States Congress is the country's legislative branch, or legislature, the branch of the government that makes its laws. It is composed of the House of Representatives and the Senate, making it bicameral, meaning it has two parts. The Senate has one hundred senators: two from each state. The House of Representatives has a total of 435 members, with each state getting a number of representatives proportional to its population. Washington, D.C., as well as the American territories of Puerto Rico, Guam, American Samoa, and the United States Virgin Islands have delegates who represent them in the House, but these delegates do not have any voting rights in Congress.

Since the word *congress* means to come together and meet, the convening of each new legislature every two years is called a *Congress* and numbered chronologically. Each Congress is made up of two sessions: the First Session in the first year, and the Second Session in the second. For example, the 2008 election will be for the 111th Congress of the United States, and the First Session will be held in 2009, the Second Session in 2010.

The Senate and the House of Representatives both meet in the United States Capitol, but generally separately. Occasionally they will come together in a joint session, when a concurrent resolution is required: an agreement reached together and all at once. *See also: delegate, representative democracy, separation of powers, term limits.*

United States Electoral College: Established in principle in Article II of the United States Constitution and further delineated in the Twelfth Amendment, the United States Electoral College is the group of people from each state who cast the vote for the president and vice president of the United States in response to their state's popular vote. Here the term *college* means a body of people acting as a unit. There are 538 electors total. The number each state receives is calculated by adding the number of senators (always two) to the number of congressional representatives a state has, which is dependent on population. Therefore, the minimum number a state can have is three, while the most populous state, California, has fifty-five. (Washington, D.C., though it has no congressional representatives or senators, also has three electors.)

As set forth in the Constitution, each state decides how to choose their electors and how they will vote. Most often they are chosen at state party conventions.

In the majority of states, once the popular vote in each state is tallied, all the state's electoral votes go to the candidate who won the popular majority. This is a plurality voting system. Once 270 electoral votes come in for one candidate, that candidate can be declared the winner, even if all the states haven't reported their final tallies. If no candidate receives a majority of the electoral vote, the president is elected by the House of Representatives. This happened in 1800 and 1824. The electoral vote decides the election; therefore, one candidate may receive the majority of the popular vote nationwide, but the Electoral College votes will go in the other candidate's favor and he or she will win the election. This happened in 1876, 1888, and in 2000.

Because of disillusionment over perceived unfairness in the current electoral system, there is a movement underway in several states to split their electoral votes in proportion to the popular vote in the state, or proportional representation. The argument is that the Electoral College would then better represent the popular vote of the American people, reducing further disputes in the election outcome.

However, if you're starting to wonder why we don't just do away with the Electoral College altogether, it is safe to assure that without this system, candidates would concentrate only on large urban areas and ignore sparsely populated rural regions. The Electoral College system ideally makes the process more of a grassroots one, with the states—especially the smaller ones— being very important at the national level. *See also: plurality voting system, swing state, two-party system.*

voting precinct: The subdivided area of your community, based on address, which determines which polling place you will go to.

whips: Whips make sure that fellow Congress members in their party are present to vote on important bills, thus securing the party platform that has been decided on. In other words, they whip them into shape! Just like there are majority and minority leaders in both the Senate and the House of Representatives, there are majority and minority whips. In both chambers of Congress, a whip ranks right below the majority or minority leaders of his or her party. *See also: majority and minority leader, two-party system, United States Congress.*

An Overview of the United States Government

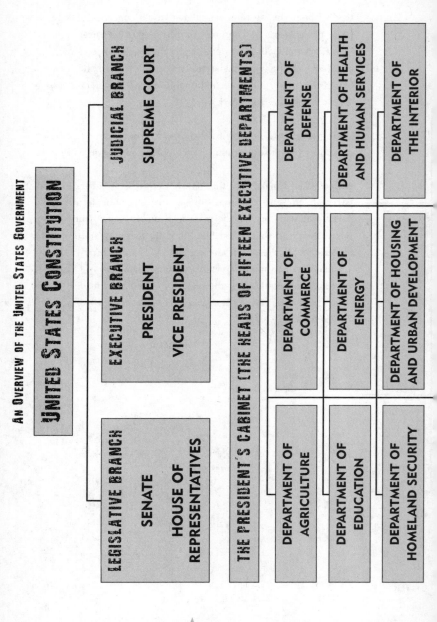

UNITED STATES CONSTITUTION

LEGISLATIVE BRANCH

SENATE

HOUSE OF REPRESENTATIVES

EXECUTIVE BRANCH

PRESIDENT

VICE PRESIDENT

JUDICIAL BRANCH

SUPREME COURT

THE PRESIDENT'S CABINET (THE HEADS OF FIFTEEN EXECUTIVE DEPARTMENTS)

DEPARTMENT OF AGRICULTURE

DEPARTMENT OF COMMERCE

DEPARTMENT OF DEFENSE

DEPARTMENT OF EDUCATION

DEPARTMENT OF ENERGY

DEPARTMENT OF HEALTH AND HUMAN SERVICES

DEPARTMENT OF HOMELAND SECURITY

DEPARTMENT OF HOUSING AND URBAN DEVELOPMENT

DEPARTMENT OF THE INTERIOR

DEPARTMENT OF JUSTICE	DEPARTMENT OF LABOR	DEPARTMENT OF STATE
DEPARTMENT OF TRANSPORTATION	DEPARTMENT OF THE TREASURY	DEPARTMENT OF VETERANS AFFAIRS

INDEPENDENT AGENCIES AND GOVERNMENT CORPORATIONS (SELECTED EXAMPLES)

Central Intelligence Agency (CIA)

Commission on Civil Rights

Consumer Product Safety Commission (CPSC)

Election Assistance Commission

Environmental Protection Agency (EPA)

Equal Employment Opportunity Commission (EEOC)

Federal Communications Commission (FCC)

Federal Deposit Insurance Commission (FDIC)

Federal Elections Commission

Federal Labor Relations Authority

Federal Reserve System

Federal Trade Commission (FTC)

National Aeronautics and Space Administration (NASA)

National Archives and Records Administration (NARA)

National Endowment for the Arts

National Science Foundation

Office of Government Ethics

Peace Corps

Postal Rate Commission

Securities and Exchange Commission (SEC)

Selective Service System

Social Security Administration (SSA)

U.S. Trade and Development Agency

United States Postal Service (USPS)

And many more . . .

BIBLIOGRAPHY AND FURTHER READING

Books

Boyers, Sara Jane. *Teen Power Politics: Make Yourself Heard.* Brookfield, CT: Twenty-First Century Books, 2000.

Christelow, Eileen. *Vote!* New York: Clarion Books, 2003.

Eldersveld, Samuel J., and Hanes Walton, Jr. *Political Parties in American Society.* Second edition. Boston: Bedford/St. Martins, 2000.

Katsaropoulos, Chris. *Every Vote Counts: A Practical Guide to Choosing the Next President.* Indianapolis: Que, 2004.

Lindop, Edmund. *The First Book of Elections.* New York: Franklin Watts, 1968.

Maisel, L. Sandy. *The Parties Respond: Changes in American Parties and Campaigns.* Boulder, CO: Westview Press, 1998.

Saffell, David C. *The Encyclopedia of U.S. Presidential Elections.* New York: Franklin Watts, 2004.

Samuels, Cynthia K. *It's a Free Country! A Young Person's Guide to Politics & Elections.* New York: Atheneum, 1988.

Severn, Bill. *The Right to Vote.* New York: Ives Washburn, 1972.

Skolnick, Solomon M. *The Great American Citizenship Quiz: Can You Pass Your Own Country's Citizenship Test?* New York: Walker & Company, 2005.

Soe, Christian. *Comparative Politics.* Eighteenth edition. Sluice Dock, CT: Dushkin/McGraw Hill, 2000.

Steins, Richard. *Our Elections.* Brookfield, CT: The Milbrook Press, 1994.

Sullivan, George. *Choosing the Candidates.* Englewood Cliffs, NJ: Silver Burdett Press, 1991.

Watson, Robert P. *Counting Votes: Lessons from the 2000 Presidential Election in Florida.* Gainesville: University Press of Florida, 2004.

Websites

Adler, Ben. "How significant is '08's youth turnout?" Politico.
10 February 2008.
www.politico.com/news/stories/0208/8418.html

Curry, Tom. "What role for Democratic 'super-delegates?':
Governors, senators, state chairs, and even Bill Clinton get
automatic vote." MSNBC. 26 April 2007.
http://www.msnbc.msn.com/id/18277678/

Future Majority website. www.futuremajority.com

Nather, David. "Leaping Voters In a Single Bound." *CQ Weekly*.
25 Feb. 2008. http://public.cq.com/docs/cqw/weekly
report110-000002675899.html

"The Online NewsHour. Generation Next: About this Project"
website. www.pbs.org/newshour/generation-next/about

"A Portrait of 'Generation Next': How Young People View Their
Lives, Futures and Politics." The Pew Research Center.
9 Jan 2007.
www.people-press.org/reports/display.php3?ReportID=300

United States House of Representatives. www.house.gov

United States Senate. www.senate.gov

"U.S. Electoral College." Office of the Federal Register. National
Archives and Records Administration website.
www.archives.gov/federal-register/electoral-college

USA.gov website. www.usa.gov

"Voting FAQ." Declare Yourself website.
www.declareyourself.com

The White House website. www.whitehouse.gov

"Youth Turnout in the Primary Campaign." The Center for
Information and Research on Civic Learning and
Engagement website. www.civicyouth.org/?p=265

"Youth Voting Quick Facts." The Center for Information and
    Research on Civic Learning and Engagement website.
    www.civicyouth.org/quick/youth_voting.htm
"Youth Voter Turnout Increases in 2006." The Center for
    Information and Research on Civic Learning and
    Engagement website.
    www.civicyouth.org/PopUps/FactSheets/
    FS07_2006midtermCPS.pdf

ACKNOWLEDGMENTS

The publisher gratefully acknowledges the following for their enthusiasm, dedication, expertise, good humor, and great speed.

✪ At Declare Yourself: A huge thank you to Aviva Rosenthal! Also to Marc Morgenstern and, of course, Norman Lear.

✪ At Bragman Nyman Cafarelli: Kevin Gessay, Daune Cummings, Scott Floyd, Rachel Snyder, and Doug Piwinski.

✪ Additionally, for their detailed editorial work, legwork, and creativity—Suzanne Harper, Robin Roy, Ruiko Tokunaga, Veronica Gonzalez, Tom Ward, Melissa Dittmar, Cristina Gilbert, Paul Zakris, and Sarah Cloots.